BORDERS POETRY

Before, After And Beyond

Richard Hammersley

Grosvenor House
Publishing Limited

All rights reserved
Copyright © Richard Hammersley, 2021

The right of Richard Hammersley to be identified as the author of this
work has been asserted in accordance with Section 78
of the Copyright, Designs and Patents Act 1988

The book cover picture is copyright to Richard Hammersley

This book is published by
Grosvenor House Publishing Ltd
Link House
140 The Broadway, Tolworth, Surrey, KT6 7HT.
www.grosvenorhousepublishing.co.uk

This book is sold subject to the conditions that it shall not, by way of
trade or otherwise, be lent, resold, hired out or otherwise circulated
without the author's or publisher's prior consent in any form of binding or
cover other than that in which it is published and
without a similar condition including this condition being imposed
on the subsequent purchaser.

This book is a work of fiction. Any resemblance to
people or events, past or present, is purely coincidental.

A CIP record for this book
is available from the British Library

ISBN 978-1-83975-639-9

*For my wife Marie
and daughters
Suzanna, Clara, Marika and Ingrid*

CONTENTS

Borders 1
   GATTONSIDE 3
   sunny uprising field 5
   TRANQUILITY 6
   HOME IMPROVEMENTS 7
   The Lamb of God 8
   The Test 16
   Commuter lady blues 18
   SMALL SKY COUNTRY 19
   Mahatma 21
   Harrods food hall 24
   HERE 26
   PAINT 31
   ANXIETY 34
   ARTIFICIAL INTELLIGENCE 36
   The way of the AI 40
   Imagine if the border became a border 42
   WIRELESS 43
   Vista 45
   for thirty years 46
   Days 47
   Bird fight 49
   Bird fight II 52
   Screwing hermeneutics 54
   THE WOES OF LAWYERS 56
   Peaches 57

Couple watching	58
Days before the pandemic hit	59
Silence	60
All you people	62
Exercise	64
Marie's chicken and spinach curry	65
Shells	67
The edge in the Lammermuirs	69
MUSSELS	71
My wife is so hot	74
English literature is essentially about coming to terms with death	76
Marie and me	77
Black and white	79
Haiku	81
Snowshoes to cutlery	95
Of what I wish to write is silence,	97
SEA AND BREEZE BLOCK	98
WALKING	100
AT THE BALLET	101
JOHN	102
REMEMBERING NORTH AMERICA	103
BORDERLINE FRACTURE	106
COMMUTING BACK TO HEATHROW AIRPORT	108
MEMENTO	110
AN OATH FOR POLITICAL CANDIDATES	112
I had a nightmare	114
AD-VICE	115
i have this image in my mind	118
AFTER THE WAR	120
HOGMANY 1992-93	121
students climbed up on the bus	122
a kilometre from the estate	123

DINING OUT IN CHABLIS	124
NINE YEARS ON FROM 1984	125
oh in Caledonia the monitors	127
During an illness	128
the moment	130
STRAIN	132
I've been jaggin	133
HALF A CENTURY AFTER	134
DEAR BUREAUCRATS	137
CHASSIGNELLES	139
POLITICIANS	140
EASY MONEY	142
ANOTHER WORLD	143
sweet sliding in the dead of night	145
sitting here wondering what to do	147
Talk	148
check in at one	149
wee hours	150
SPEED BONNY MOTOR	152
GOD IS IN THE DETAILS	153
pain of the body	154
Swimming resembles sleeping	156
Cats Like Plain Crisps	157
INTERLUDE	159
there is a lot of living in fear	160
A MYSTERY OF THE EXOTIC WEST	162
THE DEAD SOLDIER'S MARCHING SONG	164
PORKY PIG	166
FOR THE TREES	167
FOR PHAEDRUS	168
SHUSWAP BLUES	170
SHELTER	173
BIG CROW FLY	175
AMNESIA	176
as a city dweller	178

babies	179
CARS IN WESTERN NORTH AMERICA	180
well here i am again	183
EFFICIENCY	185
this is for all the men	186
MEDITATIONS ON LEADERSHIP	187
THE CONTRABLUES	188
The sun is taking a whitey	189
WHY I AM HERE	190

Technical notes ... 191

The Fear of Winter ... 192

PROLOGUE	193
THE FEAR OF WINTER	194
INPUTS TOWARDS A SITUATION	196
UNLOCK THE HIDDEN POWERS OF YOUR MIND	206
SUFFICIENT EMERGENCY SECURITY MEASURES	215
THE DEPLOYMENT OF ETHICS IN MODERN WARFARE	223
ADEQUATE RESPONSE CAPABILITY	224
NOW WHEN I W AS YOUR AGE	231
COPING WITH STRESS - A SEMINAR	237
LEADERSHIP POTENTIAL	244
TO RECAP	248
NOTES	249

About the author ... 253

Borders

GATTONSIDE

ululating silence
from ploughed
ochre hills
headlit
channelled
into parallel
unwoven hedgerows

Gattonside 4:45 am
speaking nothing
under laptop-bag black
where the stars
wonder to point
at the golden croissant
… overwhelmed by street light

Gattonside 5:30 am
beyond relief from
all drab housing
enlivened by
a gleaming pillared
temple front
I don't pray much

escape into
blueing sky
yet the stars have gone
west west again cross
the hidden depressions
yellow perfuses the horizon
crayola smear of orange

uncountable trees
stripping of leaves
tired sudden cows
illuminated dip
to passers-by
rapid mouse across
descent turn turn park

SUNNY UPRISING FIELD

chilly wind
 overlooking turbines
 spin   so   slow
two dogs flat out
chasing
 no hare today

TRANQUILITY

rust
   and gold
leaves
       spray
west
              to east
dense
 evergreens
undulate
   and sway
crow glides black
  sideways
smoke coloured
        clouds flee
vees, ayes also
double
        yous of geese
have
    departed
weeping
black
      elderberries
  cherry
the gravel
  the stones
haws bloodily explode
snug
  silent
double glazing

HOME IMPROVEMENTS

I am sitting in a room full of ladders
With nowhere to climb.
I am not speaking, nor painting.

The sun was shining then it rained
Pointlessly and without effort.
The blocked gutter dripped vertiginously
Reminding me of my homeowner chores.

The dog wagged his tail and barked
So the rabbits ran to their warren
Which surrounds us; their small
Hearts beating inaudibly below ground.

To the front of the home also
Through the pipes; running water.
The brass knobs are lacquered to gold,
Magic or trickery; I who can choose
Falsity for wise reasons may reject
Truth very much like a fool too.

So I am reclining on a bed beside ladders
Which I cannot climb down.

THE LAMB OF GOD

An improvised work for 30+ voices.

The work will sound best with probably at least 30 and perhaps over a 100 voices, plus conductor. The model for the improvisation is a flock of sheep. The improvisation should occur in a large space, or its electronic equivalent. Participants move around the space.

Each participant is assigned a unique voice. A list is overleaf and sound files will also be provided to illustrate the voices. Participants wear uniform bland white dress – disposable sterile overalls for example – that is homogenous and unfriendly but not too menacing. Additionally, each participant has a three digit number on their back and front, which is large enough to read from 2 metres away but not from 10 metres. Up to 4 participants have the same number – analogue to ewe and her lamb or lambs. Prior to performance each participant knows their number and the unique sound of the ewe or the lambs' voices.

Each participant also has a character, of their choice, and one or more moods during the performance, again of their choice. They vocalise and move about as described below, listening also to the vocalisations of other participants.

The performance has several sections. Entrance and Exit occur once. Finding & Wandering, Browsing and Avoiding can occur more than once.

Entrance

As participants enter the space one or two at a time, in no particular order, they utter their vocalisation randomly at fairly rapid tempo. Different participants use different tempos. Once all have entered, change to finding and wandering.

Finding & Wandering

Each lamb wants to find the ewe with the same number. Each ewe wants to find her lambs. Ewes and lambs find each other by vocalising and listening to hear the unique cries of those they seek. This involves not all vocalising at once. They move towards the cry until they can see the number. Then they stay together for a while. After that while, lambs begin to wander off again vocalising occasionally. Once they are separated, the finding phase begins again for them. So, across the entire ensemble some are finding and some wandering.

Browsing

Develops gradually from finding and wandering. It is a more settled phase where no wandering occurs and vocalisations have no specific purpose.

Avoiding

Occurs as an interruption to Finding & Wandering or Browsing. Some sort of audiovisual event occurs (which may be a different event each time avoiding is repeated). Participants move away from this event, which can be static or itself moving, vocalising heavily. Once the event is over Finding & Wandering resumes.

Exit

Is the same as avoiding except participants move away from the event and out of the space.

Voices: Ewes use lower pitches and more gutteral timbres – Lambs higher pitch and smoother timbres. Each participant has a unique voice that does not vary in length, pitch or timbre, but does in speed of repetition and volume. 159 voices are listed, but more variations are possible by pitch and timbre variations. The ewe and her lambs do not necessarily share the same voice. The choice of voices for a performance should not be too systematic.

1. ah
2. aah
3. aah
4. aaahu
5. aaaahu
6. aaaaahu
7. ba
8. baa
9. baaa
10. baaaa
11. baaaaa
12. baaaaaa
13. bah
14. baah
15. baaah
16. baaaah
17. baaaaah

18. ma
19. maa
20. maaa
21. maaaa
22. maaaaa
23. maaaaaa
24. mah
25. maah
26. maaah
27. maaaah
28. maaaaah
29. maaaaaah
30. ha
31. haa
32. haaa
33. haaaa
34. haaaaa
35. haaaaaa
36. ga
37. gaa
38. gaaa
39. gaaaa
40. gaaaaa
41. gaaaaaa
42. ah-ah
43. ah-ah-ah
44. ah-ah-ah-ah
45. ba-ba
46. ba-ba-ba
47. ba-ba-ba-ba
48. ma-ma
49. ma-ma-ma
50. ma-ma-ma-ma

51. ga-ga
52. ga-ga-ga
53. ga-ga-ga-ga
54. eh
55. eeh
56. eeh
57. eeehu
58. eeeehu
59. eeeeehu
60. be
61. bee
62. beee
63. beeee
64. beeeee
65. beeeeee
66. beh
67. beeh
68. beeeh
69. beeeeh
70. beeeeeh
71. me
72. mee
73. meee
74. meeee
75. meeeee
76. meeeeee
77. meh
78. meeh
79. meeeh
80. meeeeh
81. meeeeeh
82. meeeeeeh
83. he

84. hee
85. heee
86. heeee
87. heeeee
88. heeeeee
89. geh
90. geeh
91. geeeh
92. geeeeh
93. geeeeeh
94. geeeeeeh
95. eh-eh
96. eh-eh-eh
97. eh-eh-eh-eh
98. beh-beh
99. beh-beh-beh
100. beh-beh-beh-beh
101. meh-meh
102. meh-meh-meh
103. meh-meh-meh-meh
104. geh-geh
105. geh-geh-geh
106. geh-geh-geh-geh
107. uh
108. uuh
109. uuh
110. uuuhu
111. uuuuhu
112. uuuuuhu
113. bu
114. buu
115. buuu
116. buuuu

117. buuuuu
118. buuuuuu
119. buh
120. buuh
121. buuuh
122. buuuuh
123. buuuuuh
124. mu
125. muu
126. muuu
127. muuuu
128. muuuuu
129. muuuuuu
130. muh
131. muuh
132. muuuh
133. muuuuh
134. muuuuuh
135. muuuuuuh
136. hu
137. huu
138. huuu
139. huuuu
140. huuuuu
141. huuuuuu
142. gu
143. guu
144. guuu
145. guuuu
146. guuuuu
147. guuuuuu
148. uh-uh
149. uh-uh-uh

150. uh-uh-uh-uh
151. bu-bu
152. bu-bu-bu
153. bu-bu-bu-bu
154. mu-mu
155. mu-mu-mu
156. mu-mu-mu-mu
157. gu-gu
158. gu-gu-gu
159. gu-gu-gu-gu

THE TEST

On a train this morning I devised a Test
Of the elementary goodness of people
Would they surrender me to the Nazis
Or whomever shall or has surpassed them?

This Test has sparrowed across my awareness
Many, many times in my life usually
When people who ought to know better
Are spouting shite of some kind or other.

I am proud to say that my wife shall pass
My children would do their best but are beguilable
By impressive stuff such as laws and truths
That people tell you whilst becoming all serious.

No, no, no I hear you expostulating, no
Of course I would not give anyone up
Least of all someone blameless as your good self
Well is that entirely right now is it?

Shall we take the test I am an educationalist
So I will explain what is required to pass
A complete fail is of course to shop me on purpose
In case it helps you save yourself or mere distaste?

A borderline pass is that at least you would
Not actively give me up although circumstances
Would very probably prevent you from offering
Any actual help whatsoever for entirely understandable reasons.

A reasonable pass is that you would make some effort
To dissimulate and divert the armed persons from grabbing
Their victim without judging the deservedness of the victimhood
Good you would be good enough good.

An outstanding pass is that you would
Violate policies practices common-sense
And your own self-interest in order to prevent
The arrest because you would intuit the wrongness of it.

I am sorry to say that from what I have seen of people
Not many shall pass.
Nothing personal of course.

COMMUTER LADY BLUES

Sitting at my kitchen window
watching the trains whoosh by
Long time coming
gone in the blink of an eye

Well the red ones are cross-country
the blue ones are for London town
I been rushing so much lately
don't know how to slow down

I'm a commuter man baby
ready for real long ride
If there are no vacant seats
let's jiggle in the foyer outside

Heard the steam whistle holler
thought it was my mind
a green locomotive was huffing
slow grinding down the line

Sitting at my kitchen window
wondering when it'll come again
leaving white clouds floating
off into my blue blue dream

SMALL SKY COUNTRY

I used to live
   above big sky country
   were South below
     as it should be
   being Scottish
   or Canadian
immigrants to the prairies
   often flinch
and cower inwardly
   beneath endlessness
     which stuns us
hundred mile drives
   getting nowhere
     between blue above
        dun undulation below
sliding across the bench seat
   to change driver
     without slowing down
        the 605 cc engine
humming humming humming

the borders
   small sky country
changing incessantly

   clouds cruising
   across multicoloured sky
hills
   here
         and there
and there and there
green grey brown dun ochre
different dialects
   every 20 miles
its sunny
its windy
its raining
its shadowlessly overcast
   we need a new weather word
      grauh
sunny
sunnywindy
windy windyraining grauh
raininggrauh
   now it will soon be dark
spotlight sunny dazzling
purple grauh blackness
   the North Star alone
pursues us home
   from rugby training
the sky drops like a pin

MAHATMA

Was merely
   a grey tabby
kitten
   found
 living rough
 by the
   dog catcher
Somehow
   he turned up
in my wife's arms
Feral cats
   cannot be tamed
Mahatma
   took us to his heart

With striped fur
   like warm breath
he would
   climb delicately
   on to my knee
mewing
Once
   when we had been
     camping
     for a week

he did this as I sat
   on the toilet
for such
   was his love

He could sense
   cat haters
sought
   their knees out
     at parties
stared carefully
   into their eyes

Fully grown
aged about 15 months
he vanished
   into the Canada winter
After 3 months
   I threw out
   his cat chow
There was a meow
   at the back door
He manifested delighted
had lost half an ear flap
   to frost bite
his coat was
   dense as a lamb's

After that
   he settled into the
   neighbourhood
he would spring
 on to my knee

and point his head at me
   to remove claws
embedded in it

He grew huge
   did hunting allnighters
ate mice
   on the back porch
tormented
   the landlady's
eight chihuahuas
   staring down
    in green scorn
from the fence

When we had to return
   to the UK
we rehomed him
at the Samaritan's branch
   down the street
   established and housed
    by my wife

I have never
   been back
but I know
   he is still there
him
   or his children
staring
   at people and dogs
How
   and why
    do they
love us?

HARRODS FOOD HALL

copper brass marble
double expresso
   sipped slow

Earlier
in the drizzle
walking the wrong way
along Brompton Road
saw one of the bikes
   as I retraced
   my wet walking
passed the Ferrari dealer
   primary colour cars
      warm bright and dry
         behind glass

A notice by one said
      Sold Please Do Not Touch
a spray of last night's puke
   ran across
      the pavement outside
         rain washing away

sipped slow
   lavish display case
for people able
   to extrude money
      or credit anyway
staff wear black
   or white if cheffing
clients wear black
      or bright ornamental stuff
   or both
      It is warm and dry

Outside South Ken tube
   a man sits cross legged
under a sleeping bag
   shouting
"please help me, please help me"
   I give him
      a wide berth
         as does
      everyone else

HERE

There is
  no
branch
  of Harrods
in Grantshouse
even the garage
  shut down

Before then
  it had
    The
most
  expensive petrol
in the area
  basic food
    rolls milk
      soup

My daughter's friend's dad
  complained
about the price
  of petrol
the owner said
"I have to pay my mortgage"

"Not in one go"
Quipped John
soon after
   it closed
   the house occupied by
Mr petrol station owner
   closed

He still had fingers
 in the transport cafe
   pie
eventually the house sold
even the garages that
   derelict
had gutted the village
are being renovated

But no not Harrods
miserly spirits
   have money
I was waiting
     a long time
for an expresso
at the coffee bar
an anxious
   youngish guy
with artful grey hair
   tried to order
takeaway coffee
"We don't do
   takeaway
you need to go
to the bakers
   outside"

said the woman managing
   the bar
"Why
   are you being
so rude
   to
     me?"
stressed toyboy
 whines
storms off

His Daddy
   calms him down
"We'll sit in"
he admits
Upstairs I spot him
trying on
thousand pound
   jackets

In Grantshouse
we wear fleeces
   designer gear
will
   get trashed
by rough weather
Rain that can
   blow sideways
Wind that shifts wooden
   Garden furniture

In Harrods
   there is no weather
      but the virtual
   tinkle
   of money
I wandered amongst
   sensory overload
for an hour
   must buy something

The toy
   department
is a set of corridors
      and alleys
with considerately
hired
   multi ethnic
young folk
   demonstrating
toys
girl in hijab
   all in black
      on illuminated roller skates
Ukrainian-looking guy
      throwing mini drones
up in the air conditioned
      air
at the till
   beautiful
young London

Jewish guy
    more than the look
    it is the accent
It is London
    nobody cares

Around Grantshouse
    the
        occasional Pole
        the family
    who run
the Chinese takeaway
    my daughter
        claimed to be Jewish
    unchallenged
        exotic
another's friends
call me
    Jesus
Make up your mind

PAINT

I have gone over
   to the Glasgow
   West End Flat
to try to master
   my pain
which has gotten
   the better of me
   once again
problem
   Reading hurts my neck
   Typing hurts my neck
   Those are the main things I do
Although I am not as stupid
   as to be inactive
      most of the time anyway
I have been reading
   and typing today
Marcel Proust
Volume 2 also
"Managing PAIN
   (its red not capitals
   but you get the idea)
Before it manages you"
Various emails and shit

   Now this poem
This poem that starts here
   after a needed preamble
Listening to Pharaoh Sanders
   the Anti-Colonel of Afro-futurism
and the Ritual Trio
Suddenly I notice
   that at least with current lighting
the walls of my room
are remarkably similar
to those of the room where
I became an adult
Cabbage White
   becomes a pale green
Less dope is being smoked
Only I am here
Which I used to dream about
For I was a popular teen
Although or because
All I wanted to do
Was read books
Sitting in my friend's
mother's olive brown
velvet armchair
that Simon gave
to me when his mum
split for Dublin
Waterpipe to hand
Folk would drop in
We talked about shit
often intellectual shit
Stoned to Dollar Brand
now Abdullah Ibrahim

Donald said
"Wow that guy really
goes to some place"
And Pharaoh Sanders
the announcer says
is really about love
Colin came one evening
carrying a giant
shop window display
Heniz Lamb Garni tin
Which I kept
as a table
I treasure a drawing
that Simon did
of the chair and the tin
Oh
   the management
of pain

ANXIETY

anxiety,
the nebulous fronds of somnambulant events
produce wakefullnessless.
dreamed crisis,
ineffectuality of reptile tears to repulse --
that which must be kept --
activity.
keeping going on under personal strain of cogitation.
still nighttime heat of gas
radiant breath of love inadequate
for chill from fingers innards.
a tight grip upon the covers'
edges leads to cramps and throbbing temples -
anxiety.

anxiety,
the stamping run of large insubstantial horror
through landscape from childtime cartoon,
big n black n white.
understanding that running is worsening the tale-
chase yet running whilst lying still.
dry helpless mouth
but powerful rhetoric of wakeful futility --
a need to explain --

for it is that, from myself,
i demur from
scrawling the demon dream hoping
that it has been drained -
anxiety.

anxiety,
explosion of morning sunshine noise becomes menace.
explosion of personal point,
creative fear making
anger towards partner which circles
and returns to roost on the unshoulder of the
nothing which i pursue
in pursuit of me in sleeplessnessless.
the point of
falling,
the reasoned reason,
the edge of the bed.
racing brain from nose to noise to nowhere,
fear of movement,
necessity of what -
anxiety?

ARTIFICIAL INTELLIGENCE

Let's be digitally
And microscopically clear
Natural intelligence
Would be a really good idea
My friend Barrie Condon
A physicist
Thinks humans are too stupid
To comprehend the Universe
We fantasise AI shall sort this out
With what result
Currently gender orientation
Can be identified by your face
As Cecil Taylor said when "outed"
How can a three letter word
Define my identity
Consequently perhaps
AI will stay in service
To our dumb human needs
Instantly spotting who
Wants sex with you
Managing your intake
Of intoxicants
For most pleasurable effect
Scoring money for a fee

Or perhaps AI
Will be the health Auntie
Following the first law
So you will live forever
Or as long as possible
In moralistic bliss
Man how your bones
Will ache
But what time frame
Would AI take
What spatial positioning
What order of magnitude
Here possibilities explode
Should she focus on Gaia
The world
Wipe the hairless chumps out
Do it now too many of them
Are lost and destroying
So pray Ms AI doesn't read
Doris Lessing's science fiction
Should she focus on the Universe
Roll out the fine Armagnac
Cocaine and deep brain stimulation
Nothing that shall happen
On this tiny planet
This tiny galaxy
Matters not a jot
Let Donald bugger
An Ecuadorian
Nice piece of ass
Let England
And Eton
Suck off the English

Have fun live life
Iain M Banks
Saw this
The culture's AIs
LIVE
Or maybe she
Will figure out
That matter is a
Temporary energy
Flux or vice versa
And the entire
Reive of humanity
Its needs and
Exacting requirements
Shall just vanish
Immediately
All this
Whatever it is
It's not up to you
Natural intelligence
Would be
An extremely
Urgent idea
What's the odds man
You SEEN the inside
Of a University classroom
Recently
Maybe the independent
Geniuses shall save us
But they lack training
In what Jason Ditton
Called the verities

And need wonga
Loans to proceed
Icarus glides up
In my head

THE WAY OF THE A1

Whenever you overtake one
there shall be another

Tractors work hard
but cannot hurry

A fool is always the first
to discover black ice

BMW drivers can
see in the dark

In adverse weather prefer
rear end death to loneliness

Deer do not spring out
in bright sunshine

Keeping one traffic law fixedly
forgives your other trespasses

The vehicle with the worst tyres
determines snow speed

Lorries deserve to be seen
but do not dazzle us with LCD

If I am awake Macdonalds is open
but do I dream of them

To go faster it is necessary
first to slow down

Few people drive
the car they deserve

Ten miles at sixty
is as good as a rest

IMAGINE IF THE BORDER BECAME A BORDER

between Scotland and England
Not just a selfie opportunity
Already Brexit poses those problems
for the island of Ireland
Imagine if the border were a border
Living here it seems unlikely
we zoom back and forth so lightly
eyes do not wrinkle at Scots notes
until well past Newcastle
On some routes one switches back
and forth like the Tweed itself
There is still weird stuff
Lorries need drive at 40 in Scotland
much to the chagrin of A1 cars
You can buy alcohol before 10
in Berwick but not four miles north

WIRELESS

As a boy abed
with sinus troubles
I listened to the wireless
It was a big
wooden cabinet
with a dial that listed where
all the stations were
inside the open back
you could see valves glowing
John Peel and
the Home Service
Aux input

I got a record player
my Dad housed in a
homemade wooden box
plugged straight
into the Aux
Wheels of Fire
Story of the Blues
Then I breached
the open back
wrapped bare
wires round

the speaker terminals
rigged up a
big external speaker
on sale in an electrical shop
I passed by coming
home from school

Now I am sitting
still blowing my nose
Streaming New York
Jazz Radio
through my phone
into a Bluetooth speaker
And I no longer need
a radio license either
Wireless
donations welcome

VISTA

from the late train
the faint image
of a rainbow
was visible
in the far distance
nobody seemed
to notice
my seat mate
ate a banana

FOR THIRTY YEARS

I've been wrestling with
ee cummings
   i love my body
   when it is
   with your body
eventually
i love my body
i love your body
i can feel us
together entire
one body within
two bodies
i love our body

DAYS

(For Philip Larkin)

No day is exactly the same as any other
especially if you see the dawn and sundown.
Progress is infinitesimal but eventually
absolutely everything alters. Every day
it is your job to try and steer the alterations
whether this is a matter of one tiny stagger
after another or diverting ever so slightly
the unwanted boulder hurtling downhill.

Maybe the days improve but we are crippled
with memory which makes the old days
seem better for to stay almost sane we forget
the grimmest bits of them. We cannot recall
those hours of torment they were simply lived
painfully then not remembered. Sad people
get stuck in such hours. Swamped down by them
they struggle to enjoy the sunrise or the gloaming.

How do people who have barely suffered find pleasure?
How do people with no need to search find repose?
Maybe ask a gardener because poets lack the answer.
Life has to be about living it cannot be entirely about

Death yes death death decline death death death death.
Maybe we find repose in our children or agonising worry.
Every day is different from every other yet all have some
shite and some good stuff don't blend them into banality.

BIRD FIGHT

Yesterday
for the second time
I saw a hawk
take down a crow
the cunning of it

Hawk hovers high
above rookery
in the pine trees
kree kreeing loud
as possible

one angry crow
arises to chase it off
stupid bird will never
discover the power
of a mob of crows

Hawk silently flees
Crow pursues far
from the rookery
away from help
ready to prey

Or punish anyway
the diminutive hawk
Crow is closing fast
one peck should
settle the matter

Hawk stalls climbs
three metres somehow
Crow flies below it
Hawk drops to
talon blow Crow

Once, climbs again
and again pounces
they sink groundwards
From far away
I know how this ends

For first time
I was much closer
saw the merciless
struggle in the air
crow evading stunned

Hawk hitting blow
upon blow on it
until Crow fell
and became merely
a meal for pecking

I could tell also of
how the buzzards
hunt crows in pairs
which is another tale
but why "dogfight"?

BIRD FIGHT II

I was not going to tell
the other tale but
yesterday a
few days later
than a few days ago
another crow was
battering into
a buzzard
beside the same rookery
the buzzard tried to flee
crow was too quick
easily outmanoeuvred
the larger bird
which finally escaped

buzzards hunt in pairs
one hovers low above
the trees calling scree
scree
scree
very much higher
where the eye can
barely detect it
hangs the other

when the crows
battle out from
their nests
the first buzzard
flaps away slowly
leading them on
the second crash
dives a straggler
or to rob a nest
behind their backs
should opportunity
be absent the two
soar away on
the thermal uproar
to hunt elsewhere

SCREWING HERMENEUTICS

I nearly lost my mind because
my copy of JH Prynne's Poems
had disappeared from the shelf.
Well, actually, Marie had taken
it to decorate the Glasgow flat
the spine being a nice yellow.

I went to a Nichiren Buddhist
meeting once I will not recite
words that I do not understand.
My friend Ken almost ordained
as a Buddhist priest this year
then backed out always academic.

Whatever Wittgenstein wrote
we think not only in syntax
and semantics; touch the thing
the thing itself. See it. Feel it.
That is just about achievable.
Understand it? Well yes and no.

Always academic always open
to the entirety of wholeness.
Not crosswords nor any words.
Little patches paths and glimmers.
Loads of maybe well sort of floats.
It will be nailed down soon enough.

Why the urgency to sort it now?

THE WOES OF LAWYERS

So I am in a hostel in the Himalayas
Trying to get the internet

On two gee

When this guy
In national dress
Tells me there is a call
For me

It's from Palo Alto
The client wants
An immediate opinion
About a settlement

So had his minions
Phone every hotel
In Bhutan until
I was found

I should holiday
On the moon or something

PEACHES

It was the first time
George my father
Had been back
To Germany
Since he was 14
In 1933.

We were meeting
The few relatives
That he had left.

On the way
In a Vauxhall station wagon
Suddenly he stopped
On the road
Bought peaches
From a roadside stall
Smiling like a boy.

They exploded on
The tongue.

COUPLE WATCHING

Waiting for a train
Many men play
Joe cool
Assign Wifey the
Worry role
Only nag at the
Buckles of their
Man bags
While she
Arranges the idea
Of sandwiches
They glance
At the departures board
to save
Each others' glances
Oh when
Are they going

DAYS BEFORE THE PANDEMIC HIT

Stocked up for Brexit
Nothing fancy
Flour beans lentils
And fill the freezer
Just as well panic
Pandemic clearing shelves
Worry about one thing
Another walks in
Hello death
Are you not the point
Of literature?

SILENCE

What cannot
  be said
Must be passed
  over
In silence
Or babbled
  and fabled
About all along
  the wireless.
We are just
Three people away
  From everyone else
Keep two metres
 Separate.
Talk about
  The management
of Silence.
Talk too much
  To adjust for
Lacking touch.
Pray for a giant's
  Shoulders
To foresee

Forever.
If the
Earth
   Could speak
Would it be
in virus.

ALL YOU PEOPLE

Better listen to me
I'm gonna make you stupid
Just to set you free
You want your ice-cream
And you want your cake
And you want your news
Just as long as its fake.

Stick with me
And it'll be all right
Cash and freedom
Every night
You did not like
The rule of law
Vaguely nostalgic
For what went before.

When Johnny Foreigner
Knew his place
When you had won
The human race.
Freedom means nothing
In a free for all.
The likes of us
Should be in control.

But the wind blows high
And the wind blows low.
You're pushing a truck
Through the warming snow.
You voted me
For I had fuel
But you can't get any
That would be too cruel.

All you people
Who listened to me
I made you stupid
And set you free.
I got it done
Built my estate
But you can't come in
That's inappropriate.

EXERCISE

Three military helicopters roar low across the field in loose formation
Machine guns dangling insouciantly limp from their doorways
Painted in tasteful grey camouflage for Eastern Europe somewhere
Not a human in sight within the buzzing machines where are they going
The dogs who chase sparrows, rabbits, badgers, hares, hawks, geese
Apparently could not care less never glancing up at the whirligigs
But continuing to play fight beneath a sight that could terrify
in a different time and place I reassure it is a training exercise
Jets I have winced at before but helicopters are a new addition here
I am sure it is entirely a coincidence in the chaos of almost maybe
Brexit will it really extend to civil unrest in the Scottish Borders?

MARIE'S CHICKEN AND SPINACH CURRY

I have been making this
for 23 years
at least
once a week
it is one
of the reasons
well my cooking
in general
why we
remain together
when we
were dining
on our own
it made her
feel nurtured
she can ask
for the curry
to be exactly
such and so
consequently
it has evolved
once the children

were tucking in
it also
gave a sense of family
and continuity
to Friday evenings
participated in
by their friends too
who sometimes
had never had curry
or homemade curry before
Richard's curry they said
but no
it is Marie's

To begin with
I followed a recipe
Out of a book
Madhur Jaffrey's probably
Slowly it improved
more tomatoes
add potatoes
cook them first
more turmeric
some Kashmiri chili powder

SHELLS

Nibbling a wee scallop
   Leftover in tomato sauce
The doorbell rang
My parents' friend stood
in a fawn overcoat
A black bin bag in
   Each hand
'I thought Mary would
Know how to cook them' he said
   Coming in
The bags were crammed
with dripping
   palm sized scalloped shells
My father invited
Pip's two pals up
From the car
My mother pulled
Mrs Rombauer
Off the dresser
Adults drank whisky
The bath rinsed scallops
The hall smelt of bladderwrack
I wondered if I
   Would like them

On the half shell
With onions and wine
Monday night au gratin
Tuesday with tomatoes
   I did
Then they were gone
Until now when
  They are all gone
So I rinse
the empty ramekin

THE EDGE IN THE LAMMERMUIRS

Wind turbines
   are
a trinity of scimitars
   coloured
like Chinese death
   sucking
money from air.
   Nary
a sound but
   piped
water hum.
Ruining the imagined
   countryside
with Anthropocene
   fingering.
Without electricity
   where
would we be?
The same was said of
   oak woods.
Simultaneously fast
 like
missiles;
   slow

like oars;
   invisible to sheep.
The twelve I walk
   between
are far ahead of us.
Enormous however
   unobtrusive
everywhere yet
   hidden
within the hills
reducing the neighbours'
   bills.
We have sold on the
   human
landscape for one hundred
pounds a quarter.
It is not
   natural
never has been
the whole
   ambience
reeks of human being
and red diesel.

MUSSELS

Hang
   in clusters
are hard
   to dislodge.
The blue rope
Is all
   they've known.
Gently
   they bubble,
They filter trash news,
   moan unheard
in false harmony.
Under threat
   they
Clamp shut.
They yearn
   for the
      free swimming
Days of Spawn.

Prawns
   mean nothing
to them
   Pinkies eat
The wrong food,
won't bow
to the fool
nearest the surface
who eats
   the most shit
 would get fattest
but for the strain
   of being
on top.

When
   the starfish
shows up
   he's
the first
   to go.
The others
   can't move
   a muscle
Or undoubtedly
   they would
show
   their love and esteem.

One day the rope
   will be pulled up
   and it won't be
   their fault.
After all they
      Always
   snap shut.
Now that's how
   scientists run
      a department.

MY WIFE IS SO HOT

my wife is so hot
when she walks
down the street
harmonicas rhythm
her sway

my wife is so hot
when she talks
the black bird
awakes turns night
into day

my wife is so hot
when she hums
all the clouds
astonished they
scatter away

my wife is so hot
when she takes
off her boots
restaurateurs have
nothing to say

my wife is so hot
when she sits
up in bed
the weans curl
up and lay

my wife is so hot
she listens
and hears
receives gifts of wine
and crochet

my wife is so hot
when she walks
down the street
harmonicas rhythm
her sway

ENGLISH LITERATURE IS ESSENTIALLY ABOUT COMING TO TERMS WITH DEATH

attributed to JH Prynne

meandering through the byways
of north Northumbria aiming
towards in the near distance
the chill blue North Sea
no satnav no phone signal
sometimes the sea looms
above a leafy ridge
then it vanishes again
discovering unexpected things
a sail-less windmill
two snails, the flash
orange of a weasel
ming of a badger
inevitably I shall get there
after lingering in sunshine
in the end why hurry

MARIE AND ME

We changed into wedding suits
hastily in the back of the car
parked underground by
Kensington registry office.
Witnesses two old friends.
Luckily one brought bouquets,
found a jobbing photographer,
whose photos fade lovingly
framed on our windowsills.
Our marriage arrangements
were impulse but our love
never has been such a thing.
Grand wedding plans sunk
below parental indifference,
even scorn and yes fear.
So, we did it ourselves there
scoffed oysters, flew to Venice,
holed up in a tiny hotel room.
Marie was unwell with clams
being five months expectant.
Oh, it was grand, grand, grand.
The big splash that would not last.
Yet it did four daughters three
grown women themselves

and our love that continues
due surely to our foibles and fancies.
Yes, we still have the suits wardrobed
and the shoes kicking about
in some cupboard somewhere.
Certainly, we can't button them up,
but still the linen feels like love
and now we wear silk pyjamas,
cuddling in bed, foot-rubbing,
watching the sun enlighten us.

BLACK AND WHITE

They say I am always here
at my desk on the computer
but in reality I am barely
here at all scarcely present.

This afternoon I was in Hull
collaborating on this, that and other,
emails to and forth and back.

Then I spent a while in China
commenting someone along with
their English written sentences.

Then I attended Scottish Parliament
consulting about the Good Food Nation.
Deep fried crème egg anyone?

Tomorrow I shall be in Austin
taking a discursive harmonica lesson
gazing at a resonant room.

They say I am never here
because I have literally disappeared
into the abstract written domain.

My words assemble into sentences
which are surprising to me
for they say that I am quiet.

Yes as silent as a magpie.
And there you have reality
the full reality of it
in cold black and white.

Haiku

FOR SIMON

No-one allowed long hair
yours flowed
far below your shoulders

Everyone had long hair you
wore tweed
got a short back and sides

*

Rain drops raining
Haggis is on top of tattie scone
Heaven

*

Small fit grey man
The branch almost
Smashed his ankle
Aw fuck

*

Ruby Diamond Gold
Dark dual carriage way
Ruby Diamond Gold

*

FOR MICHAEL RUBIN

Every breath across
each reed and hole
different learn them

*

Toilet paper bumph
Cannae get enough
Until it floods up

*

Allium pink stands
shocking while
small beech leaves fall drab

*

Something up we're
Up for it. No?
We flow flat into dogs mat.

*

Soaked through at back
Autumnal beach tempest
Front sand dry

*

I have nothing to say
Why am I writing
I am high falling leaves

*

Unable to choose feelings
Dusk wets teatime
A thirsty page

*

It is the gloaming time
missing you
please turn your ringer on now

*

Sager psychologists than me
Say nothing ends well
Even this

*

Pruned from where dykes gape
rough cairn
Drystane labour

*

Sprout tractor illuminated
Santa's sleigh
Three sleeps Halloween

*

Cloud factory plume
In thirteen years
Not once the same

*

Ungainly breaststroke
In azure ripples
Of lithe children

*

Morning haiku
Look here
A child of five
could do this

*

An anthill
Of people
Black winter coats
Central Station

*

Reservation system crashed
Congested aisle
Just sit down

*

Hay bales drying
During rain
Unexpectedly ploughed umber

*

Dirty old Autumn
Mundane bushes ablazing
In holy spirit

*

What is the scenario
Where railway police
Need riot vans?

*

Raindrops rain
Rain drop ssss rain
Rain rain drops rain

*

Delay train fault
clear announcement
I don't inhabit Crewe

*

Below St Pancreas
Books like Benito boxes
No poetry

*

Three guys in kilts
Share a haggis
Supper in station

*

Mechanical arthritic
Rain radiant nuptial heat
Duvet day

*

In the doghouse
Nowhere else to go
It's warm dry known

*

Inorganic er
Spinach now what the fuck
Is that gimmick

*

New school
Chatting homewards in rain
blossoming with spirit

*

Icicle winds
flooding but now light
at five pea em

*

Plastic playhouse
In horse trodden acre
Of mud for who

*

Cold cold chill
Indoors snug fleece
Piano song

*

Dog play fight rip
Her face off in
Mindlessness

*

Thousands car
train through here
Yet remote

*

Distracted by the
Telly the Haiku it's
Gone or is it

*

No two sauces be
Ever the same
What a world wonder

*

Optician said I
Years on would see much
Better double it

*

Conde Nast traveller
Suddenly that world
Vanished gone

*

Red camilla early
Flowering clear
Silent times

*

Shimmer of hammered
pewter big moon spring
tide silence sweeps

*

Moonshadow
Duck quack a
Harbinger of her doom

*

Lift dogshit one
nine flower primrose
imposes the lawn

*

Coronavirus

That word again and again
and again in lambing season
Wagtails swish in silence

*

Isolated walking for exercise

Collapsing grey drystane
Mottled with lichen
Startled with lime nettles

*

Murder of corbies crawin
For small life
Or new carrion

*

Light light headache
pounds sun swallows
Swerve over sky

*

Badger trucks calmly to
Us on the road
Sways into grass

*

The patio table
Yellow sun hat flattened
Thundery rain

*

Sun cools
Poem lasts blink
Of an eye or two

*

Drifts of beautiful
Shirts enrich me
I glow in the taleoring

*

Why does the weasel
Jump jump weasel
Does why?

*

Swallows evaporated
Stubble dry chino
khaki shadowless

*

Friday thirteenth
Her lucky day I won two
thirty on Euromillions

Snowshoes to Cutlery

OF WHAT I WISH TO WRITE IS SILENCE,

five ways of it.

The roaring quiet of lodge pole pine
a hundred meters afraid above Kananaskis camp
exposing the generator of my blood.

Awake, bank holiday dawn when
neither trains, myself, nor the incinerator arise
through the dew with the damp sun.

Reading behind the tee vee blaring
and her staring at the screen with the peace
of unimportant events passing.

The high hum of overloaded cochlea
wobbling on Lothian Road after a tardy electrified Lifetime
had blowed the Calais down.

Yapping dog now calmed in garden
no cars on the road past the hill top village
the ruzz of crickets a footstep.

Nothing can not be written
five ways or none.

SEA AND BREEZE BLOCK

1.
on dark gray sand
rowed white loungers
blue plastic cushions
the sun arcs the volcano
the interminable ocean
is multicoloured, empty
dangerous currents
at about three quid a day
we bask, snack, even read
the towel dwellers below
come and go, splash at
the edge of the infinite
smoke theatrically nude
the high rise town is irrelevant
'till tea-time, abendessen

2.
road falls over dark cliff
villas perch road falls
around and down
and around 'n down
there is the sea breaking
white banging breaking

there is a large block of flats
modelled from east Berlin
tumbled concrete outhouses
protect the car park and behind
the pastel flats built under
the final diagonal of the road
a bus coughs and slides down
the roof. Three people get off.
There is a tunnel to the beach
it has collapsed. Firm above
a pink villa has been built
out on hideous concrete buttresses.
A radio echoes from the bar.
We are drawn to the swimming pool
molded in a rocky sea cove
The surface spumes gently
as high waves fuck down its side
and smash on the concrete wall.
The wet salt is exhilarating.
Two older women swim attentively.
Waves have bent the guard rail
but only rustle spray the pool.
We watch waves fall and devour
nothing, damp basking,
for over an hour.

WALKING

above Aguamanista we were walking
high over the black beaches
way behind the azure Atlantic
above the pine trees we were walking
raising caking red dust eroded
on the knees of the volcano
above Aguamanista we were walking
beneath the layers of lava sun
high over satin floss clouds
beyond the weather we were walking

AT THE BALLET

the harp is tuning slowly
while girl children
eye the stage
before us dates
fall in love
she lowers a
stiff arm across his shoulders
he smiles but only
leans in during act two
by the clog dance
her head is under his chin
everyone lives happily ever
after strawberry ice and rose petals
mother has a heart after all
and even the fool loves
his red umbrella

JOHN

you would sing sad songs
i don't know where
you found the time
now you say
'I've forgotten how
to play them'
no time
no sadness
no stave across
your wide forehead
relaxing with your new spouse

REMEMBERING NORTH AMERICA

Putting down Proust onto my lap
an image of TV
in some irrelevant horror movie
but from the desert
brings it all back.
How each building
as with this abandoned white clapboard
church framed in my living room
stands sharp dry and unique
against the blue sky and the
immense imperceptible horizon.
I have an urge to describe landscapes
perhaps I will see myself
reflected in those unpeopled places.

As when at dawn on
a mountain ridge
shadow streamed west
across the dense dark valley of trees
making form across the silent mist
drifting westwards upstream.
A stick broke a mile away
above the hiss of brownstream's water.
I stood ears swivelled

into the dawn echoes drowned
in the pine tree line.
Someone was making a fire
for smoke rose in a strand
up to the sun I turned
my shadow swung out and
bobbed gigantically downward
as I soft-footed back to camp.

Another time in the Seven-Eleven
the security video showed my profile
in swarthy high contrast
before cutting back to the doorway
along its blind routine.
On the doorframe was a height chart
to gauge or discourage cheats and robbers
or more likely the oil-fingered kids
who hung out across in the catalogue store
parking lot sitting on the hood of an
old Ford Maverick or in the back of
Dad's Ram pickup newly washed for town.
They sucked on ice-slushes of coke or
lime and waited for friends to drive by.
Sometimes someone left the lot
blowing inky rear-wheel rubber
on the gravel left from winter.
Later on too tired to read but TV off
I caught a beaten reflection
in the grey screen and wondered
who was left in the lot in the dark.
I imagined the punctate glows
of smokes or grass from BC and

slight conversation while across in the store
the night clerk watched herself
in the monitor as she swept up.

That is the way I catch America;
suddenly from a corner of mind's eye.

BORDERLINE FRACTURE

>   It should be easier to go to
>   your neighbour
>   than to go to the moon

Berlin Wall graffiti: 1989

The old mind set is stirred if not shaken.
'Men, we must proceed with caution
in these new times.
Assuming they are really new...'
Hooded blind sight.
Capitalist apologists juggling clichés like pinballs;
polished and shiny everyone scores something
when the big bells accidentally ring.
The right is a matter of emotion.
'Greed and panic are good, yes?'
At least there are signs of life
in the old individual yet.
Will the heroes of the 20th century
be the people who said 'We were wrong?'
Some governments, closer to home
would rather be burned at the stake
than admit that.
Respect for the individual
means we must tolerate

any eccentric old rubbish
as a sign of our leaderships' strength.
Language is limited in the right brain -
swear words, platitudes, a few childhood nouns -
it is the emotion that counts.
Experts with the power of speech
cannot state the trashy obvious,
lefty bastards they smarm out everything
into linear epoxies of words;
abolish hanging, be nice to people,
don't give drug dealers ten years.
It does no good to anyone.
Fuck that, 'Get tough on litter louts'
the right brain yammers 'Blame someone, punish
someone its not my fault'
trailing off into a grammar school whimper.
'I really didn't burn the toast.'
Remember: They are going to thrash someone
and it might as well not be you.
The left finds it hard to respond
to these absurd intuitions.
It struggles for words.
Yea - now who is easier to read,
Marx or Archer?
That puts the writing on the wall.
Pornographic slogans replace reason.
Get your tits out for the lads,
you sweaty red bitch.
Bloated yet hungry, enterprise sucks

COMMUTING BACK TO HEATHROW AIRPORT

(in New Writing Scotland 1993)

the worn old train was dust
it fluttered above South London
in the damp heat sweat stuck
my shirt to the seat of dust
below buildings were falling
and building at the speed of earth
prim landscapes were bursting
out of back gardens along the track
a great copper beech once
a focal feature of a lawn was
bending a fence and smothering
the weeds beneath it dog roses
competed for track side
with hedge bindweed
pink petals with a daub
of yellow stamens white trumpets
a bower for not sleeping
the train creaked
over beautyless drab terraces
the white man leaning on a sill
had dreadlocks 'Pay no Poll Tax'

the bill was on recycled paper
in another garden a ragged wash
fluttered over rusted old things
nettles and much more bindweed
creeping into Clapham station
there is a green gap by the track
where some industry fell down
or had been pushed aside
bindweed yet hardly hedges the wire
fence through which I see
a grand red and dun dog fox
digging for worms or beetles
paws pushing at the soil
panting for his city livelihood
the meaningless train pulls me away
to hesitate for no reason outside Victoria

MEMENTO

She came from her converted grain mill,
paid out on Visa, got on a plane quick,
eager to chip a small piece from the wall.
Bringing along for the purpose a neat ice-pick
with embossed silver plate wearing off the handle
and a convenient plastic bag made by Zip-loc.
She wore gloves to keep her manicure fresh.
All that was needed was the littlest, tiniest
attractive portion of the wall for the mantelpiece;
ideally a clean chunk about the size of a book.
She had her school-girl phrase all rehearsed,
'Bitte, ich möchte nur eine kleine greifbar stück,'
in the hope that some lad would provide the muscle:
'Dear lady, no of course it is not too much trouble.'

But when she had pushed to the decorated place,
the crowds of alien jabber were too much for her
and she slunk off in the dusk to a meagre space
where there were broken bottles, a burned out car
and rusted grimy concrete finishing off the terrace.
She felt that it was sehr verboten hack a scar there.
So the secure lights of publicity drew her back.
Now it was peaceful, even the guards were at dinner.
She found a nicely coloured crack and, leaning in, struck

a stylish but ineffective, silver-plated blow.
With a shudder the crack became a great gap.
Change had not been her intention. Ah so!
Luckily hundreds had pounded there before;
no-one could say that it was all down to her.

So, now there was a view she leaned in to have a nosy,
holding her mane aside, squinted vainly with one eye
to see what she could see as the dust settled. Funny
it looked like that bit of the city she drove through
every day on her route to the office back in her country.

AN OATH FOR POLITICAL CANDIDATES

(as proposed during the Conservative Party Conference of 1985 to prevent the election of terrorists to public office)

I SOLEMNLY SWEAR
    i SOLEMNLY swear
IN FRONT OF HER MAJESTY THE QUEEN
    in front of her majesty the queen
AND ALMIGHTY GOD
    and almighty god or whoever is listening
TO AVER AGAINST THE USE OF VIOLENCE
    to aver against the use of violence
IN ALL ITS FORMS
    in all its forms
FOR POLITICAL PURPOSES
    for political purposes except as shall become
    necessary
    during my term of office (if elected)
    specifically
    such police and military action as required
    to protect the values of our society
    as embodied in the decisions of any
    democratically elected
    government of which i may or may not be a part

as well as
any emergency measures deemed necessary
by peace officers
or other agents of the crown
in order to preserve
law and order
> furthermore i agree not to resist the
> restriction or arrest
> of any individual (including myself)
> if this becomes essential
> for the safety
> of the realm

I HAD A NIGHTMARE

and woke up screaming
I was making a speech on TV
and no-one was watching me
but I went ahead as planned
what else can one do
in front of the cameras
it is well-known that
under the appropriate circumstances
with considerable artifice
the camera can
tell the truth
but no-one was listening
but I was dreaming

AD-VICE

Somehow, they said-
    in a voice
    which was
    not quite singing
    but not really whispering
    any secrets
        in those synthesised plosives
        which as planned
        aleatorial background
        have come to present
        finance and corporate success-
you have
to raise the cash
for this.

So I loaned my arms
to the casino.
Somehow, they said-
    straightening
    the tie of silk
    which resembled
    polyester in its mediocre
    striped shimmer

        in the burnished bronze
        washroom mirror
        where blue eyes became
        as black as damsons
        drying in a sterile sun-
you must
permit them to
like you.

So I left my wits
by the TV set.
Somehow, they said-
    smelling of gin
    beneath amplex
    over too-hurried
    oral hygiene and telephone
    sanitisation fluid
        smelling of wool in summer
        and rare beef
        made acrid with chillies
        and the back seats
        of long-waiting-list cars-
you should
invest your money
wisely.

So I purchased shares
in an arms dealer.
Somehow, they said-
    unhurriedly
    replacing the
    tiny dictation machine

      in the jacket pocket
      of the inner jacket pocket
          where thoughts lay
          cushioned on fine linen
          like saintly relics
          of the most painful kind
          blessed and signed wholesale-
you better
speak your mind at
the right time.

So I auctioned my library
for their charity.
Somehow, they said-
      extracting undigested
      but hastily faxed
      annual projected percentages
          prepared by my white-nosed
          be-shirt-sleeved
          animalistic rival
          from the data which I
          had painstakingly collected-
you haven't
realised your full
potential.

I HAVE THIS IMAGE IN MY MIND

an image of a man and two children
on an old settee watching television
late in the evening
or should i say not watching
for the man he
is slightly drunk on beer
and the kids are playing
with Galactor and his
mutoid battleship which
at finger's flip becomes
then unbecomes something
like a mountain lion but
with the hindquarters of an ass
(have the lion and the unicorn
fused at last) on the television
Sir Robin Day conducts election
question time where three suits
one with frills two without
express their varied distress at
the inability of them theirselves
to resolve the issue of women's rights
in education in this country
the man he is slightly drunk on beer
and does not really hear the speeches

the wife is out cleaning a **PR** firm's office
if he were watching at all
he would have turned the channel
although later on it was shown that
this particular programme was pivotal
in deciding the outcome of that election

this image puzzles me
what can it possibly mean
a tipsy man, two children
a space being, a lion a unicorn
Sir Robin, three suits
and an election must all
be the work of my imagination

AFTER THE WAR

MANY INNOCENTS HAD BEEN BURNED
AND, AS TIME AND TIME BEFORE,
THE WRONG PEOPLE WERE CONCERNED

HOGMANY 1992-93

These bells I was alone
but Tara phoned
from work with wishes.
Then the wind began to blow
like a broken harmonium
humming Amen.
I waited with one whiskey;
no-one came.
A gale chapped the door
chanted the patio furniture
and reeled with the fence.
It seemed something was ending
or starting.

STUDENTS CLIMBED UP ON THE BUS

boisterous and clear spoken
laughing at their own jokes
the YTS kids
slid stern glances at them
old women flapped their ears

innocent and confident
o let them laugh
happiness is rare

A KILOMETRE FROM THE ESTATE

downhill from the yellow farm
there is a rabbit warren

among bramble, rose and thorn
the far streetlights glimmer
like candles in the misty dawn

i see a fox for the second time
swerving from my sight
into the browned rose-bay willow herb

brown fox
brown stalks
its gone

DINING OUT IN CHABLIS

The huge inert moth on the path
resembled the pebble dash dust of it.
Black speckles on its pate
protect from birds and
even us, for deterred
by the memento mori vaguely displayed
and the bird-size of this moth
we do not prod it to life
(if it still lived).

Brushing the dust from out feet
we sit above the side
canal, limpid with algae.
Geraniums spray from
the old water mill's window box;
mauve and white.
Hovering in from the dusk's
initial calm comes the huge moth,
wings figure-of-eighting in a blur
like a humming bird.
An eight-inch thread
tongue tups each bloom
leisurely. It departs
we sip Kir, awaiting dinner.

NINE YEARS ON FROM 1984

you should not read Jung late at night
or maybe it was the morsel of cheese
anyway i was lying in the silent dark
with closed eyes
when my voice spoke
'i want to live' it said
'so what is killing you' i wondered
'that is for you to know'

oh i know
this country is killing me
with its slick yet grudged viciousness
the rationality of grammarians
no wonder it takes a Chomsky to see
beyond the block-building logic of America
but the British Chomskys
have already flown
from the rain, The Sun and
the wireglassed bodgers in their dens
who run things here

what is killing me is
the need to become someone else
in order to succeed

old farts call that maturity
being half dead from their own fears
and quite young in years
many of them
they'll bring you down to their level
pox their faces with gin and gravel
on their sea-change patios

'now who,' I wonder
'just who, the hell are you
to be beyond that?'
my mind is alive and priceless
midst the permanent post-Christmas sales
my mind is flipping over
like the leaves of a station clock
my mind is hijacking a locomotive to sunwhere
for it takes dreams to survive
among all this in this time

OH IN CALEDONIA THE MONITORS

of tapes from mall cameras
send courting couples flowers
and vouchers for fine china
in Caledonia

security personnel assist shoppers
with their bags encourage kids
to zap the latest games for hours
feed runaway waifs in the food court
then offer them work as sweepers

oh in Caledonia the border
has been Hadrianed over
by Merrie Old England plc
the Celts shall be free only
in Caledonia

border agents wave across wire
encouraging Geordies to immigrate
their mortars lay down leaflets
picturing the idea of social services
and the standard rates of hire

oh in Caledonia

DURING AN ILLNESS

Williams' vision narrowed
to an idiotic picture
on the wall
i too am sick
but of the soul

my colleagues' voices
hustle by me
echoes in a tunnel
my sisters' worries
scrap the air
far off gulls

'Welcome to cyberspace'
where abstract tanks converse
and shoot to overload
[the next level
what is the point
of it all]

oh it is a little screen
on a little world
which repeats
with variation
again and
again

comforting

THE MOMENT

was there to be seized
rather than bless-
you'd at
the moment
the fruits of perhaps
months perhaps
no time at all

the moment
was dark and white
redolent of street lights
and breathing
breathing
the moment
blood keens in the night
of a universality
clear as wine

the moment
is far unforgotten
yet memory is not the point
reason slides
into membrane

the moment
of a flush of touch
unexplained
sustained in hush

STRAIN

o
i began
to straighten out
when
the great ache
of my back
      snapped
    then
i collapsed
  at
  their feet

I'VE BEEN JAGGIN

I just wacked it in
now it's rolling right over me
fuck the polis
fuck the law
fuck ma da
an fuck ma maw
fuck the social
fuck the school
up here in Possil
smack rules

droppin jellies
tae bring on the stone
back a ma face there's nae cunt home
fuck the jail
fuck the doc
fuck the telly
fuck the clock
fuck that AIDS
fuck the hep
am I fuckin deid?
no the yet

HALF A CENTURY AFTER

the liberation
of Auschwitz,
    even
the raw timber
buildings
remain in place.

Bones and tombstones
    will be there
much longer.

This was a massacre
    that we
can still remember;
we have industrialised
    everything
smoothed, perfected, cheapened
production,
    life and death.

Only
    the spirit
cannot be mass-produced
our vanity
is to believe
    a mourning plaque
will alter us.

Yet the individual agony
    of gangrene
from a sword thrust
may be worse
than that of forced labour.

The cameras map slaughter
in primary colours
whereas the hell of,
    for example,
    Bosch
is merely a painting
    or perhaps madness?

Our sin is to think
that we know the truth
and, wise,
would not be so
    sullen nor tearful
as those German burgers
staring aghast at
the accounting
of nationalism.

These days the work camps
    are run by foreigners,
starvation is a personal choice
while genocide is
    leavened with charity
for the greater good
    as always.

DEAR BUREAUCRATS

I address you bureaucrats in rhyme,
as for my prose you lack the time.
My letters sent, though well-composed,
melt away like paper snows
and when the spring comes by your pen,
you solicit my answers yet again;
'Please address these questions soon,
so that the great plan can resume.'
The plan, the scheme, a mighty willow,
that draws its moisture from our marrow,
seeded in sub-committees where
trees flourish without earth or air.
Hydroponics is the gimmick now,

shown by some gardening business show,
you study-toured at our expense:
No soil, nor space, savings immense.
The nutrients cost a bomb it's true,
but lacking them we should make do.
A tree must grow, this tree must grow,
the ancient bird will make it so.
Glossy squawking goads the folk who toil
to fan the air and tend the soil,
inspires them to cart away that muck

and build new glassy boxes up.
Boxes where sprouts could climb and thrive,
if only some were still alive.
In the trampled earth forgotten seed
disorders back as bright fire weed.

CHASSIGNELLES

First on the right
   is the Rue Emil Prudhon
one turns left along
   the canal side
wild apricots bloom
   by the road
the restaurant's patron
   will vote against
   further unification
from fear of an erosion
   of frenchness

POLITICIANS

politicians
don't tell lies
just sometimes awkward facts
slip the government's eagle eyes
they deny the past
shutdown the state
make education training
so we won't learn who to hate

if there are
no records
then it don't exist
if it didn't make money
then it won't be missed
the church is a sham
and the state went wrong
now who is going to tell us
what the fuck is going on

you can buy off the press
you can tap all our phones
imprison the poor
so they leave you alone
you can censor the past

selling genocide guns
but you wouldn't tell lies
'cos that would be wrong

whitehouse TV
and gag Shein Feinn
do what you like
in the nation's name
security first
and drugs must be prevented
if the IRA didn't exist
they might have to be invented

EASY MONEY

easy money
comes and goes
you blow on the highs
and suck on the lows

get it on credit
get it on time
trying to make the payments
will eat your mind

unlike the standing order
the new rug will fade
thing about credit
its never out of date

the rich get the breaks
and the poor get the blues
I'm sick and tired of singing
this old news

ANOTHER WORLD

in another world
where I had no other
in another world
last night we were lovers

I can see it in water
I can see it through mist
we got a little drunk
then we kissed
in another world

in another world
where I had no other
in another world
we loved being lovers

I know all the lines
and what the band would play
that other world
was just a touch away
in another world

In another world
more than friends
in another world
I'd need no amends

but you took a taxi
and I took a hike
sorry but I'm married
and that's what I like
oh but in another world

in another world
where i needed you
in another world
where romantic lies come true

I can't see if it lasted
but I know it was good
believe me darling
I would have if I could
oh another world

SWEET SLIDING IN
THE DEAD OF NIGHT

awkward on the telephone
you turn my head
and black is white
girl I can't leave you alone

don't wanna be your footslave baby
don't want to be your fool
don't wanna hurt nobody
but I can't obey these rules

white lies they shade to grey
passionate embraces fade
what should I say?
a little death
or has death been delayed?

don't wanna get all nostalgic now
don't want time to rewind
don't wanna pile on pressure
but see if you change your mind

sweet sliding in the dead of night
awkward on the telephone
you turn my head
and black is white
girl I can't leave you alone

don't want no coup de foudre
don't want to be a disgrace
don't wanna eat your mouth babe
honey I'm losing the place

SITTING HERE WONDERING WHAT TO DO

lord you left me with the lowdown blues
sitting here just wondering what to do

well its dark outside and it started to rain
there's a hole in my shoe and i'm in pain
sitting here just wondering what to do

well i tried drinking but that didn't work
and i tried thinking but that just hurt
sitting here just wondering what to do

they say there's no smoke without a fire
you kept my love stole my desire
sitting here just wondering what to do

you can swear on the bible on your mamma's grave
woman i love you won't be your slave
sitting here just wondering what to do

TALK

    is easy
talk
    is hard
        O what
    loud-
       er
          than
    thy
word
    is there
bar
    the tell
of
    a heart?

CHECK IN AT ONE

the room is unavailable
all-day meals commence at noon
there are two cups of coffee
a bit of soap, one picture
an evaluation form
thank you for you custom
says the last notice you see

please find a vacant table
and note the table number
place your order
at the food counter
quoting your table number
pay for your food
when you order
our staff will then serve you
at your table

WEE HOURS

one AM an rain
today we
cleaned house
watched TV eke down
lottery, comedy
cowboy movie
now she snores
I should be tired
but the blood
jigs in my limbs
who dreams of what
these springing nights

*

half past one again
the heat is down
but its timer tocks
in this familiar house
a clock picks off off-beat
this year I've often
heard these sounds
still I cannot decide
do they strike a rhythm

beat to the same plan
in her bathroom
she kept that motto
from Thoreau

*

Two
As so often I snap awake
erect, tense, hesitant
I fancy some nights
your thoughts alert me
as you unwind bedwards.
The silence reminds me
of your easy blush.

*

spirals
and strange visions
men bearing spears
an arm of mine was gone
the pain had lifted
it seemed to be summer
someone was chatting
in french or spanish

SPEED BONNY MOTOR

Touring Skye
life is of salt water
only the booming roads
crack the hills.

GOD IS IN THE DETAILS

All along Dumbarton Road
   the houses of God
   are selling furniture
Jupiter, Forrest
   House of Pine
On Sunday
   families process
from one shrine
   to the next
in quest of the best.

PAIN OF THE BODY

ache of the spoken
no vows had been taken
bruised but not broken
flat on my back
the yellow dreams come
in the slime of my pain
my love became numb

i was afraid of my pain
it came and it came
i bowed in to my ills
bombed it with pills
my back was as tight
as the tyre of a bike
it went round, round
riding and falling down
then i threw it behind
with my malcontent mind

i was scared of the calm
sure the silence hid harm
so i sang high, spoke
wrote papers, joked
enterprise bought peace
for some while at least
now i struggle, i feel
despondent just to heal
i must get back on
or this love will abscond

SWIMMING RESEMBLES SLEEPING

temperate breath in the azure quilt
sleeping resembles swimming
long measured stillness of dreams limbed
migraine resembles sleeping
ridiculous aura rebores us tongue furrs
sleeping resembles migraine
being more like linen than little dying

CATS LIKE PLAIN CRISPS

Speed Kills
sanctimonious terror posters merely
wound in the interests of command

E Is For The Effects Can Last Forever
death, unpicked from the weft of life
pixilliates on the front page - scratch n ban

Heroin Really Screws You Up
o it had them in patches and stitches rags and rages
so the drug itself were a rush of nothing

Crack Is Almost Instantly Addictive
or what the big bucks it brings the agencies of enforcement,
    sure you need a chopper for
your copper to stop the glittering tides of crack Ð like that

Drugs Ruin Lives Call Crimestoppers Now
shop your noisy neighbour grass up that nosy neighbour
    evict a darkie now no not for a
score not for a fiver for the sweet sucking pleasure of it

Blow - That's No Drug
hows about suck? yea hows about a bucket if there's some
    mellow shit in it
yea yea yea grudons taht wolb

Fine Wines Direct To Your Home
delivered by helicopter (shoorly no - ed)
at substantial extra charge - the markup's on us

I Was Not Human Says Killer Addict
yet beasts have no property, rob not
and behave cruel in clear calm blamelessness

We Appear To Have Gone Down Sir
fags are a drag fags are
father brother son 'n manna to me

Do Life Not Drags
do not drags
do drags
        drags
its all
sport at the night's (de)termination

INTERLUDE

The narcissi are fading in a copper jar,
around its belly the room bends as a frieze,
small ornaments loom large,
lights shrink to stars,
the artist is as tiny as a seed.

THERE IS A LOT OF
LIVING IN FEAR

just for instance
on my parents stair the younger
residents had an entry phone fitted
to mitigate their imaginations
as they climb the worn stone steps
to their homes having quickly
got out of their cars in the darkness

just suppose this and did you hear about that
yes and i nearly died not
forty yards from my workplace
at ten a.m. when a building stone
the size of my head and shoulders
mishandled smashed on the spot
where i would have walked
if i had not looked upwards
as it toppled

very calm and very unexpected
what sensible security could
have protected me against this
or that but i tell you
i won't be walking on the pavement
past that prestigious office development
next time something
goes down

A MYSTERY OF
THE EXOTIC WEST

The burning creature came down the high street,
who was to say whether it walked or crawled
for, in the shimmer of its burning,
it could not be ascertained at all.

The heat imploded **Hi-Fi Madness**,
Giant Savings went up in gas,
the burning creature did not falter,
but continued to advance.

Inside the bankhall blue fire captured
a million banknotes a-roar in flight;
the flaming savings caught men's hearts,
strange figures aped against that light.

Down the mall the creature wandered,
indifferent of what wares broke,
in violent heat of unpassionate
strange flame and poisoned smoke.

A camera cracked, the pixels scattered,
Live At Ten died in the air,
as it had sprung, the creature vanished,
there was chaos and babel everywhere.

One witness thought it was a Buddhist,
protesting at the death of meat,
another claimed it was the Phoenix,
whose pyre was commerce's defeat.

The enquiry found it was a fire,
quite unplanned and unprovoked.
'No evidence supports a creature,'
Lord Chairman said, exhaling smoke.

THE DEAD SOLDIER'S MARCHING SONG

two days dead beneath this tree
my eyes stare up but cannot see
the burning sky above my head
the living grin between the dead
my mildew bones return to ground
hands still tight to catch the sound
to catch the sound that i last heard
a bombshell singing like a bird
there are no birds upon this tree
my eyes stare up but cannot see
the flying flag i fought here for
the tee vee glory of this war

my flesh is chewed by dogs and men
my liver's gone to strengthen them
a killer walks quite slowly past
observes my scaffold, moves off fast
my common stench goes close behind
i still reach out though i be blind
i still speak hard, though i be dumb

cry out aloud 'come soldier come
look at this work of dogs and men
my liver's gone to strengthen them'
and now my heart will never beat
the hero's tramp of homeward feet

PORKY PIG

The tangible leak of blood
smell. One eye affronting,
clouded, one small eye.

Rags of ivory fat
scattered. Thick grease here,
everywhere, thick limpid grease.

A butchery of orange gloves
moving. Small knives cutting,
stripping. Small surprising knives.

An indomitable smash of machine
chains. The radio plays
inaudibly, the limpid radio.

One still tongue slimy
red. Lolling silent out,
on concrete. Lolling dead silent.

FOR THE TREES

The back of my guitar is made of spruce
wood while the front is made of cedar.

Playing 'Namia' by John Coltrane i view
through the window two large trees
bursting with red berries.

I do not know the names of the trees
in the garden across the road in the city.

Neither does the squirrel who travels to the berries
on the branches which she understands step by step

in the invisible city where trees play the music
she cannot hear in between my bare hands.

Music for a stranger woman
written by a dead man
while the trees grew.

FOR PHAEDRUS

who went blind
which i noticed one day
on a walk when
he ran into parked cars
collided with bushes
and fell into a ditch
i cried for him
for he had loved to run
and still tried to
for a while
until dazed and lost
he crept to my voice
and i led him home

we had him put down
for he moped about the house
would scarcely leave the porch
and could not find the fence to bark through
so that summer when
i tried to snap the gophers
he would have chased after
walked the hills
of the wild Kananaskis alone
and watched the sun come

up over the ridge without
his distant presence in the bushes
then i said farewell
as well as one can

SHUSWAP BLUES

i woke up this morning
and it started to rain
looked across the lake
and down the clouds came
trees are green
sky is grey
give me sunshine
sunshine today
in the summer time
when the weather's sultry
i feel fine
downcast skies
and i'm cast down
it started to rain
while i was looking around
down on the beach
i saw tiny mountains
just within reach
picked up a pebble
put it back down
in the summertime
into cool water
under cloudy skies
i shook my head

and i shut my eyes
feeling the rain
flicking my cheek
down on the beach
where ripples hiss
across bits of slate
and old trees tumble
down to the lake
and one boat
kinda just rolls by
under cloudy skies
over water that shines
to some missing isle
with a little pier
out in the swell
up on the beach
some dog running
over bits of slate
to the water's edge
where wet logs rock
and a crow calls out
in the silence
that carries off
someone's shout
to some missing isle
way over the lake
under dripping pines
and budding birch
and smoke that climbs
still
still
where the wet logs rock
cupped in the hills

just below my feet
to that white line
where shore and lake meet
water is black
the sky is bleak
under dripping pines
that the ripples shake
as the rain falls in
softly
unheard and unseen
it smells of balm
and of burnt bark
just below my feet
in the firepit
where red wood runs black
and green rock
is brown and cracked
my hair is wet
but my fuel is dry
as the rain falls in
give me sunshine
give me sunshine
or give me rain
i don't mind
whatever the weather
i feel fine
i feel fine

SHELTER

any storm that breaks this way
bounces across the hills and islands from the sea
inland we are sheltered from the wind
in our newish timber-frame houses
built with extensive prefabrication
upon the marshy remains of waste ground
to the north of the city
somehow the wind still swirls about
the entire estate piling plastic potato wrappers
into dense mats of litter in mud-ridden corners
'its terrible' they say but someone's wains
must be responsible no mythical teen vandal
will walk a mile from the hill-flats to dump an
empty eighteen-pee bag of Wotsits in our flowerbeds
the cloudstreamed lemon sun skirls in
through our venetian slats with a rhythm
echoing the shattered cassette belltone of the ice-cream van
we vaguely recognise the tune but
'what's its name again' I rise and close the blinds
against the chink of pence upon Irn-Bru returns
snug in the house it's Sunday afternoon
TV? there's nothing on
we could walk hair ripped ice bald
out along the Kelvin past the Science Park

towards Bearsden in the rain
where keen golfers swat wet balls into the spate
and a glitter of magpies mimic the landing planes
or tramp over to Asda and buy something
larger than we need in a polythene box
covered in cling-film with a piece of plasticised paper
lining the bottom what's it for that paper?
if I knew that answer I would understand a lot
instead we sit tight in the house listening to the rain
I am glad we are not all at sea this afternoon

BIG CROW FLY

big crow fly
big crow fly
where then sun hangs
in a big blue sky
walk a long way
ride on home
when the wind blows
and the snow don't come
pray a long time
dream a long dream
found a stone
like a man
in a hollow tree
hollow tree
hollow tree
found a stone like a man
in a hollow tree
gave my old name
to my best friend
now he's called big crow
and i'm stone man
stone man fly
stone man fly
where the sun hangs
in a big blue sky

AMNESIA

this afternoon
i opened a document
to see what it was
a meticulously written
piece of teaching
of which i have
absolutely no memory
there were three others
all dated last June
let's see my ex-wife was ill
something or other of the heart
She was in hospital
some setback or other
we were getting drenched in Cork
eating and drinking well
buying rain jackets in a sale
walking to exhaustion
round the Kilarney lakes
She had a stroke
was never getting out
my sister leaked me
the evil 'C' word
what She was Never getting Ever
shit, with all those cigarettes

i went and took back my dog
from a house no longer mine
her sister brave faced
but trapped in weeping
She had only a few days
a visit would be useless
also against her wishes
we bathed and brushed the dog
drove the long dark drive home
must have worked and for two weeks
then She half climbed out of bed
trying to live or escape
died, i had already wept
the things you can forget

AS A CITY DWELLER

I relish
   the darkness
with a
   long spoon
in the country
my neighbours
   can't wait
after they've
locked the gates
   to elevate
great
    golden
   globes of light
blasting out
   across the
blue night
   like guitars
blocking
   the clear
sparkling stars

BABIES

arrive dead
grey
they haul in
the cool breath
of the morn
scrunching at
the light
where they've
been while
they were away
was very dark
and warm
they slough
their burned old skin
and gaze for
the lights
of our eyes

CARS IN WESTERN NORTH AMERICA

in memory of Raymond Carver

there was betsy
the blue ford maverick
with rusted bodywork
when tara drove her
from indiana to san diego
the highway patrol
let her go after doing 80
cos look at it how could
it go that speed officer
there were big holes
in the back floor
freezing in winter
terrifying in summer

up in alberta
we got betsy
fixed up our
foster son dean
and our pal harry
shoehorned the chassis

into a new white body
she sat in the back garden
dean had hoped to drive her
but by the time he made 16
she'd sat all winter
we'd sent him packing
for stealing and
breaking curfew
we sold her
for a hundred dollars
she started right up

i bought the pale blue
toyota corolla estate
for 200 dollars off a fellow
sloane scholar who was heading
back to sussex
she ran a bit rough so
the coked up metal guitarist
we were staying with
cut off the catalytic converter
saying as my dad says
if they're built by niggers
we can fix em
naturally she seized up
on the freeway
never quite the same again
she crawled through
the mountains en route
to canada
where i cracked a cylinder
tanking it back from calgary
high on prairie tedium

the car i had for two days
a fiat the kind ladas were
modelled on
the engine went on fire
we got our 200 bucks back

seventy-seven chevvy nova
two door 408 bright orange
from when cars were made of steel
bang it on a pole
suck that dent out
with a plunger thing
17 miles per gallon
think dukes of hazard
half the radiator grille was missing
could never track down a spare
only motor ever that went faster
than its speedo dial allowed
burn off young cowboys
and fridge repair men
when the lights turn
thats it
there's no moral
nor ending with cars

WELL HERE I AM AGAIN

clearing
sitting about
wanting to be elsewhere
clearing
its not the scientology thing
there's no ology at all
living
unfortunately is no ology
or osophy
clearing
a deep breath exhale hold
wait for the words to come
managing
anger people uncertainty
email deadlines mortality
clearing
for some reason the campsite
smokes into my head
clearing
deer wine water wind
chopping wood correctly
twisting
the axe very slightly as
it falls so the log splits

clearing
the old stump each side
as it unhinges
cracking
sprays red orange
palid and brown chips
clearing
onto the barky earth
echo of woodpecking
drumming
the dream of firelight
in the darkness
clearing
day

EFFICIENCY

Wheezing to sleep
under a heavy cold
the snow was coming
along with darkness
a child is beginning to stir
in her body in my mind
she is worrying understandably
about everything to come
so why do my dreams
hack up the past so hard

THIS IS FOR ALL THE MEN

who roam around the highways
of the South of England
this is for all the lonely
men who roar two yards
from the bumper of the car
in front of them
this is for all the lonely men
they want to be fast
this is for all the lonely men
they want to be hard
this is for all the lonely men
they want to be first
this is for all the lonely men
they want to be home again
this is for all the lonely men
talking to themselves
come on get off come on
talking on the phone
this is for all the men
who roam
keep me away from in front of them
this is for all the lonely men

MEDITATIONS ON LEADERSHIP

suits black suits white stripes navy obedience shoes tip
    wings fly
pixels of futility dutiful reading a local joke policies
    implementation
presence one close work glasses impassivity suits pastel ties

above the hostile audience
he leant on the lectern
and radiated a smile
in silence for minutes
until they were all laughing

THE CONTRABLUES

Woke up this morning
Didn't feel too down
My woman was a bit tetchy
But I decided to stick around
Got three children
And they all look just like me
When I get a worried mind
I just sort of wait and see…

THE SUN IS TAKING A WHITEY

above the Russian vine
Shiel is giving me
her early evening stare
the deaf old shepherd
planted calm in the garden
i have just sipped an exquisite
glass of white wine
peaches and grass cuttings
Marie's show has been
and gone at dawn
so we've been waiting
waiting for the waters
never have i felt as a live

WHY I AM HERE

my grandfather was gassed
in the Somme or somewhere
one of those muddy haemorrhages
of the great war that make the
close quarter shooting
of three or four dozen
civilians like pop-gun play
anyway he had dysentery too
collapsed in retreat at the side
of some road his brother
in another regiment altogether
found him and carried him home

TECHNICAL NOTES

My usual style of poem uses uneven feet resembling speech rhythms, which I originally adopted after William Carlos Williams, although UK rhythms are of course different. Many poems are influenced by the Cambridge School, except they are Scottish and perhaps postmodern. In my style rhymes and alliterations are used for emphasis rather than to maintain the groove. This may perplex readers schooled in older poetic structures as well as those familiar mainly with rap and poetry slams. I also write lyric poems, which are typically songs, often in 12-bar blues form, and usually rhyme in standard ways.

My English haiku are roughly within the tradition of 3 lines 15 or 17 syllables (except when they aren't) and the majority of them have an air of seasonality, in line with Japanese tradition. My attack of the haikus started after reading the lovely book 'Through the letterbox' by George Bruce, with illustrations by his wife Elizabeth Blackadder. At time of writing, I am in recovery, with minor relapses.

THE FEAR OF WINTER

Why are you watching? Someone must watch, it is said. Someone must be there.

Kafka

PROLOGUE

ice ice
clamid breath in the mouth
a ribbon of fur
that struggles to speak
bleeding nails on
inky finger-tips
and they call this writing

THE FEAR OF WINTER

sleepless and steaming
i stare at the ceiling
o when will it come down
the little sky the little dream
the little crack hands tight
over the face like that
yes it's as easy as falling
off a tree into the rich bush below
off a tree into the deserts of tomorrow

ragged and bearded
blinded by the sun sun sun
i imagine the rain should come
until my eyelids are stuck together
and crusted over with a scab that
feels as huge as it can with no fingers
no gut reaction to feel it with as
i cough with what's left of a lung
making the speech of my dreams the speech
of a lifetime of words words only

what should i say and why
should it even be said in this hallway
be said taking a piss be said
in this bedroom in this hesitation from
one place to another from one state of
mind to another via some revolution or other
i sit upright like a soldier of the night
and with my pen in hand fall right back to sleep
right back to the plains of Africa or wherever
i come from wherever i come from next time

INPUTS TOWARDS A SITUATION

a.

old water leaves
a few traces in
winter on the
open ground
and then we
dig down deep
as we must
in these times
around a hot fire
back into the
fantastic
plastic past
when men and
things worked
for us when

stones made from
sand buildings
made of stone
cities made of
oil and paper
warriors made of

air and facepaint
the world before
the words before
winter was the world
freedom in exercise
of right yes right
not night not
knight not rites not
riots in those
wealthy times
plunder sure
you can understand
that what had to be
taken was taken
and given out as
the written fist
of justice so no-one
but the hungry were
starved no-one but
the dead were dead
no-one but the speakers
spoke above the noise
of exploding gasoline
across the tree-stripped
country in the sandblasted
greenbelts called Dunvotin
and Ayegotmine Gardens

then the gardens became
torches as the cars exploded
and the radios became dead
during the emergency tribunals
while those who took anything

where shot in the open
when exercise became freedom
and warriors became air
and cities became paper
and buildings became stones
and the underground went above ground
and plastics became monuments
in those times

b.

overheated negotiation
in a frame of metal
they are driving
the point home a
hard bargain of
lives and macroeconomic
platitudes
small was beautiful
crisp paper a thin
plastic card inserted
a flexible ribbon
marked magnetically
moves above the heads
of the walkman
made in Japan cast
in concrete
the music stops
the representatives piss
and work back to the beginning

fundamental compatibility of strike capacity
estimates ability to access and rectify
as the report of a break for ice
water glancing out over lakeside
mountains and entrances to shelter
in order to maintain continuity in
order to resume with plausible haste
the investigation of motives in five languages
which boil down in the crux of the matter
to five different displays of status yet
  and we must give a great deal of credit
  to the translators
this is not discussed
tabled or reserved
for future meetings

everyone is independently satisfied
the ambience remains diplomatic
no guns can be seen a dim
saxophone warbles in the elevator
as the secretaries go down to dine
none of them is really listening

c.

after the disaster
  the crux of the affair
  is that they
which can be anyone
  give not a fuck for
  the irradiated devastated devalued statements

>   which have been done over in the name of
>   objective assessment

more and more it is the fact of the matter that
unofficially and off the record
just between you and me you understand
on camera to the nation
in fact
the leak could hardly be called a leak at all
as it was contained immediately
and produced nothing which has been shown
to cause significant harm to human beings
given the kinds of exposure which we are talking about

but which i am not at liberty to divulge
although i can assure you they border on the
insignificant
most people
in the course of a perfectly normal day
lie more to themselves than do any
forty statements
that have been made over the past forty-eight hours
whatever the opposition says
i assure you we will study all the relevant data
including the economics of the matter
to insure that such an affair never
comes to light again

>   in this way the voters will be protected
>   and the people
>   will have to look after themselves
>   at least until the facts
>   the facts are weighed

d.

all property is theft
that is unacceptable
although we submit that
property belongs only to those who
make/buy it and must be
defended against those who would
take/buy it against our best interests

by needs by force by threats
so our beliefs shall be measured
and night time is the right time
to be with the one you love
oh tell it now with the one
you love diamonds or uranium
livestock futures or oil surplus
its all cash in the account
for someone respectable
with a house or two
and a car or so
just like you
and the one
you love

so sitting silent side by side
on the special offer spring sale
sofa watching the nude faces
reading their lines across acres
of carpets and the endless line
of central nervous system depressants

you say nothing not wanting to
wreck the boat of twenty four percent APR
and plunge your lover into

the unbearable
only abstractions are deadly
death it not itself destructive
through the power of prayer
you can unlock the hidden powers
latent in everyone
send no cash just fifteen ninety nine
in four easy monthly instalments
will bring you a complete course
of the ancient secrets of the Aztec
mystics translated by an eminent
anthropologist who was in fact
the real-life Indiana Jones and
brought to you for the first time
ever in this
unlikely to be repeated offer

yes blood and sacrifice are
the answers as long as you
are not the offering so phone in
before someone else does
after all last month's prowler
never stopped by to claim his prize
and fourteen million pounds
went back into the bank
where it belongs and

believe that or you will
believe everything

to maintain its position
increase the swing velocity
of the emergency baton
and insure that the anti-personnel
shields are fireproof and
protect you valuable documents
with our fully-guaranteed safe
for without those photographs
and proofs of purchase concerning
your beloved possessions there
may be grave problems
in claiming the full amount
that you are entitled to
from your insurance brokers

meantime the police
force continue to cruise
in twos in reinforced Fords
and unknown numbers in
the vans that creep around
late at night prepared
with no expense spared
for every contingency
to protect you and
those listed as your lovers

e.

i dreamt that in one blast
the rubber melted from
ten thousand nightsticks
revealing the steel cores beneath
near the epicentre the forces

of law and order were vaporised
but soon returned
shooting at will to control
the rats which scampered
in and out of a million melted
deep freezers and across the
shadows and bones of citizens
who despite their orders had remained
and spent the final two hours
for so the cops saw from the shadows
screwing looting and
pissed as lords denying
entropy through delirium

i dreamt that someone
for no particular reason
opened up on the cops
with a machine gun
and when the ammunition
ran out the survivors
raped her and smashed her skull
while the rats darted about
and the seagulls circled

then one cop slipping back his cock
said "fuck" and fell over dead
and rapidly the others expired
but there was no time for an enquiry
all they learned was that
whatever it was
was called death
and if you got too close
then you died

meanwhile out in the countryside
the motorways remained jammed
with bodies and wandering blind
whom no-one bothered to feed
in the safer farmhouses books
burned for fuel and life cost
a gallon of petrol while everything else
was worth sweet fuck all
the government broadcast instructions
and how they were under control
but the microwaves had trashed the radios
all across the land so no-one heard
except for agents of the government
things being flipped inside out
like the guts of a cow ripped apart
by a flying girder
it was fortunate that we
were not at war
in those times

UNLOCK THE HIDDEN POWERS OF YOUR MIND

a.

anxiety,
the nebulous fronds of somnambulant events
produce wakefullnessless.
dreamed crisis,
ineffectuality of reptile tears to repulse --
that which must be kept --
activity.
keeping going on under personal strain of cogitation.
still nighttime heat of gas
radiant breath of love inadequate
for chill from fingers innards.
a tight grip upon the covers'
edges leads to cramps and throbbing temples -
anxiety.

anxiety,
the stamping run of large insubstantial horror
through landscape from childtime cartoon,
big n black n white.
understanding that running is worsening the tale-

chase yet running whilst lying still.
dry helpless mouth
but powerful rhetoric of wakeful futility --
a need to explain --
for it is that, from myself,
i demur from
scrawling the demon dream hoping
that it has been drained -
anxiety.

anxiety,
explosion of morning sunshine noise becomes menace.
explosion of personal point,
creative fear making
anger towards partner which circles
and returns to roost on the unshoulder of the
nothing which i pursue
in pursuit of me in sleeplessnessless.
the point of
falling,
the reasoned reason,
the edge of the bed.
racing brain from nose to noise to nowhere,
fear of movement,
necessity of what -
anxiety?

b.

words in the box reflect me
inside my head i whimper "stop that"
but the malignant words continue
to spread and be

reflected into the street corners
and across the backs of people's hands
in gestures and grimaces i recognise them
i choose a number and press the button
the beam will not pass
through solid objects but can be reflected
off the walls as if it were an
invisible snooker ball bouncing
from word to word
and on the other channel...
the end of a conversation
went
so you
        are a
poet
        but there can't
be a living in
        that
so how
        do you
earn your keep?
        i'm a psychologist
oh
and on the other channel...
the thin line must
force firm against
the fuzzy who-knows-what
and there can be no medal
brown enough for those
who on the other channel...
cut that out
and write it down because
in a moment i will give you

the address for we are interested
in your opinions and if you miss
the address you can find it on page
fifty-six of the system on the other channel

and so it goes
on and
the bright lights
bounce around every
living room
in the land
spreading something
to say at least

me? i'm kinda quiet at parties
but learnt in California how to
talk back to the telly
the ads especially and so i
chatter away well aware
that nobody is listening
who can hear because the box
says it all
one way or another
but press in the button and

the box is empty
we watch the dot vanish

c.

fridge
you'd better take the door off
of it fridge

which by the power originally provided
by the decomposition of one thing
to another
>   be it rainfall to the sea
>   or hydrocarbons into
>   carbon dioxide plus nitrogen or
>   some isotope to another
preserves through cold
stasis
>   as when found
>   a frozen mammoth
>   intact in a glacier as
>   when The Thing came alive
>   in canine then human form and
>   after a century or so
>   ate the canned goods
>   left behind in the ground remains
>   of Milton Keynes and
>   glowing delicately
>   shuffled off into the spectacular if
>   infrared poor sunset
yet without power
the fridge is an enticing
dark trap into which
the less mature of us
may snuggle in the hope perhaps
of being preserved but
never to awake
you'd better take
off the door better
watch out for dust clouds

watch out for power surges
listen to one thing
and another
the door opens
a light lights its
tungsten element
and spreads over the
old cottage cheese
and browning soggy
vegetable material
as nothing dark or
light stays entirely
the same it takes
energy to remain still
while chaos is efficient
and simple

out on the dump
a black headed gull
swims somewhat uncertainly
on the pool of algae-ridden rain
water collected in an upturned
freezer lacking a door
so life goes on from
one thing to another

d.

someone is cutting the grass
to the blast
of an overpriced
plastic cassette radio

the redundant
bass beat inexactly
follows the
drum machine
while interference
from the poorly shielded motor
does not seem to concern
the grasscutter
but adds a fart of static to
the July air while
with a kind of ecstasy
of concentration
i watch TV

oddly enough
a few powerless suburbs survive
and after the first winter the homeowners
pile their useless lawnmowers TV sets cassettes
food mixers battery operated transformer gobots
and all the other ninety percent plastic household items
into a communal bonfire that belches hydrocarbons
for the two minutes which it lasts
while a few tired children dance a little then
pick metal from the embers as their parents
return to the houses and continue trying to beat
their central heating systems into plough-shares

still
on the bright side of things
the attack of the giant ants
never comes around although
after the second summer our homeowners discover
that the attack of the minute ants

can be as troublesome as a mortgage
in point of fact they should never
have let the grass grow
even if it does feed
the few sheep which someone rescued
from the land outside
driven distracted
the survivors slash at the ground
with copper scythes made from hot water pipes
nobody sings much

e.

the smell of burning flesh
means that no-one feels like cooking
for a few years which is just as well
because fuel is damn scarce and besides
mouldy potatoes taste pretty much the same
cooked or raw who gives a..
even those pretty little backyard barbecues
turn out to be worth nothing because
the only fuel which will fit in them
are those nice preformed charcoal chunks
which now cost at least a chicken or a fuck
for a small sackful

some of the hardy sort build stoves from
their hot water tanks and run a chimney
out of the kitchen window
it takes several hacksaw blades and then
there is the problem of wood
loft conversion after loft conversion
is split apart that first winter

those fortunate enough to own a vented gas oven
discover that they can burn cow dung in the bottom
when there is dung to be had otherwise
they grow cold and thank god
that ski jackets were in fashion before winter began

if you upturn a drier and rip off the plastic door
then you can burn a fire inside the drum
as long as you have adequate ventilation
but many people abandon their homes
rather than mutilating them in this fashion
they say they will return when things get
back to normal but the moment they are gone
the neighbours break in and take what they need
back to normal indeed they never
come back at all

SUFFICIENT EMERGENCY
SECURITY MEASURES

a.

selected routes have been selected
as evacuation routes for the duration
of the emergency these routes will be
marked with the route markers as indicated
in the guide which each household
will have received during the week before the
onset of the emergency

if you have not received such a guide
then contact your local
evacuation route advisory council or police
station for a copy when the alarm siren
sounds do not be alarmed but evacuate the building
do not lock doors take nothing and wait for your
evacuation bus during this time obey any orders given
to you by evacuation officers police officers and keep
your radios on for further information

under no circumstances take pets or belongings
to the buses your needs will be met at your destination

which for reasons of security cannot be revealed
at this time but will be somewhere in the countryside
which has been laid aside for such a contingency
rest assured that the government has your best interests
in hand and obey any orders from
your local emergency council who represent
your government
for the duration of the emergency

such reassuring words as were read aloud and posted
all across the land which had been named the
Third Reich words to be obeyed for the salvation
of the nation should not be interfered with by the
machinations of mere individuals
especially from the subhuman sectors
of the population
in the name of the greater good
please get on the bus

the mistake made was not to arm
the evacuation officers from the beginning

b.

during the carnival officers danced
to an air of constrained relaxation
many of them would prefer never to have firearms
and fewer of them than we imagine have
needed to wield their truncheons in
the line of duty but then far be it for me
to instil an unhealthy air of reality
into the increasingly political fantasies
which our children are learning screen by
scream to prepare them for.....

a death by the unimaginable which
becomes a technical challenge
burn the bastard burn the bastard
cut his nuts off burn the bastard
we howl as he goes up in smoke yet
even the hardened retch naively
at the stench of the real thing
they toss aside their flame-throwers
bury scripts in their breasts and flee
but son-of-a-bitch there's nowhere to run to cos
the the camera crew follows so the hard men turn
to inflame the audience so we chant their chants
out into the streets

the trouble is that the streets are deserted as
neighbours crowd around TV sets
watching the deserts glaze
but ignorant of the state of affairs
in the scheme over the next hill
so they buy alarms to keep out burglars
who as they saw on a show the other night
are trained in obscure martial arts
learned from their childhoods
of hideous plastic deformities

but out cruising in the Sierra
rear end a frozen-food container
ice gran
and shred the skin of their heir's face
it was so sudden I never expected it
doing eighty-six miles an hour
that fast who expects anything
death is sudden death is dwelled upon

in intimate shots of macerated equipment
and rigid chalked corpses
this is The News

mildly jiving peace officers
turn inwards from the crowd
to seriously listen to their radios
intent officials dance to the killers' tune
once again an appeal is made
a point of law is amended
weapons are justified
for just-in-cases
while a carload
of gelignite
implodes an
office's
window
The N
ews t
his
is

.

c.

I got in a two-year supply of food
laid out on metal shelving in the basement
each container labelled with expected life
canned goods on the left please beans, peas
tomatoes, peaches, meatballs, ham and franks
freeze-dried on the right mild curry, chicken
in a deluxe cream sauce, turkey and gravy, stew
made with reconstituted soya protein and

assorted dried vegetables packed in plastic then
wrapped in foil and placed in boxes lined with
earth along with a collection of spices with which
to improve the flavour of twenty four months feeding
at the back in those tins are seeds of various kinds
and I have a select selection of hand tools
packed down in grease in the other room just
through there is our shelter with bunks to sleep
seven I intend to add another bunk soon
hidden beneath the last bunk is the false compartment
which contains two shotguns a cross-bow and a .22
rifle along with a collection of traps some grenades
five machetes and axe and two hundred axe heads
which I plan to use for trade
along with an adequate supply of ammunition and
the cartridge loader which
I picked up for a song in Brighton

suspended from the beams is a generator
which can be powered either by this treadmill
or from a petrol motor
there should be enough of them lying about
after-
wards
so I have not bothered to store one here
rather than rely upon a continuous electricity source
I have buried the medical supplies beneath this trap-
door for coolness and I am hoping that we can find a
fully-qualified nurse or even a female doctor to
join the resistance team my wife god help her
would not countenance the logical one to two
male to female ratio which I propose here although
I must admit to being disappointed by the overwhelmingly

masculine response to my adverts so far the
one I ran in Women's Realm did you see it
last week produced no response at all
still I am sure we can fill all six bunks
with suitable candidates in the end

the seventh bunk? that's reserved for the wife
when she decides to come back

d.

an unexpected consequence of
the new naval road built across
the hills towards Loch Long was
that the road rapidly jammed
with cars from Maryhill to Milngavie
and when the traffic inched to a
dead stop the pedestrians emerged
and walked slowly and strangely
unaccustomed to the exercise across
the hills past indifferent sheep and
beneath the pillowing clouds of the west
towards the submarine base

within a mile or so of the base they stopped
formed a transient encampment without tents
or cooking equipment only the odd bottle of booze
improvised camp fires and other drugs
which were at first taken with caution but
as the night wore on so hash was smoked openly
and heroin snorted by many who abhorred it
back in the city but it seemed appropriate
while waiting for the air burst which

would both extinguish and ignite for ever
each flickering flame upon the hillside

"at least it will be quick" was said
over and over across those long hours
according to someone's radio
before it was turned off by popular demand
there were riots in Birmingham, Bristol and
George Square while the South had more or less
ground to a complete standstill traffic being
backed up from Taunton to the North Circular
while several traffic wardens had been run down
by frantic Volvos trying to ensure their own
safety by escape to their personal lot of old England

after three days of intense negotiation
some people had begun to trail back across the hills
when finally the air flowed colourless and deadly
as greater Glasgow melted and by a quirk of fate
a collision or machine failure perhaps human error
only those who had waited so long to die suddenly
were still alive to greet the guards from the base
as they deserted their posts and cracked the armoury
ill-prepared but lively the crowd moved north

e.

in a cold narrow room with the hum of air filters
two humans exercise in silence
they have already said all there is to be said
and must conserve the electricity supply
for more important things than music
by the mutual rhythm of long practice they

first greet the sun stretching
in opposite directions forty-three meters below ground
hands touch floor hands
stretch to almost ceiling
hands rest at sides breathe
with slow concentration and discipline then
they do the cobra the camel the lion the rabbit
the tree the breath of fire and to finish
the dead man

which relaxes and conserves oxygen
neither of them
need to think of the names of the exercises
neither of them think much at the moment
it must be night time
this is the fifty-third day
food supplies are not yet a problem
twelve of their group are already dead

THE DEPLOYMENT OF ETHICS IN MODERN WARFARE

ADEQUATE RESPONSE CAPABILITY

a.

it was not that the ladder
> that misclassified tower
> of soft-bound documents
> taken seriously for twenty-five minutes
> then shelved for future reference

so to speak
was thrown away
but more incinerated
over the space of a few days
and when the temporary government
emerged
and looked about them
they found nothing relevant left to say
for the contingencies for their contingency plans
had failed or been misfiled
one way or the other
people without imagination
had been unable to face up to the unimaginable
and many lapsed into listlessness
just as they had before
in their offices during the
pre-lunch blahs the

quarter-to-four
its-not-worth-getting-anything-started-now feelings
and of course the famous nine a.m. blues

the trouble with handwriting everything is that
everything must be written by hand which means
that circulation must be limited unless an item
is of sufficient interest for everyone to copy it
in other words a single air-blast redefined
the processes of administration
while clearing of rubble went on
none-the-less with a few wheelbarrows
some shovels and a lot of swear words
and before authorisation could be coordinated
by the various departments - War Peace Property Health
and Interim Area Coordinator's Office - involved
rebuilding began

at first there were simple shanties of
piled smashed concrete and plywood without water
without sewage and without assurance that the
areas inhabited were inhabitable
some died some did not many investigators and
liaison officers from the above-mentioned departments
were among the causalities as
gradually the danger areas were learned
during the
emergency accommodation liaison co-ordination meeting
of June the 23rd
it was agreed that these areas would be
marked clearly in red on the new maps once the
Ordinance Survey cartographers had fully explored
Britain's new coastline

b.

the first corpse
which the hastily recruited
able bodied clean-up squad
encountered was human
and they wondered behind
their face-rags whether
it had been a man
or perhaps a woman as it rolled
into the pit slopping loosely
on the seeping oily water

by the tenth
they had established a grim
rhythm only broken when
limbs came away in their
cramped hands they swore and
began again to seek out
each others eyes
conversations picked up as
they sweated in the overcast heat

after a hundred they
took a lunch break
sharing a pop bottle of water
eating in the slow slow
way of those who will eat no more
today but do not wish to work again
calmly eating potatoes without salt
surrounded by their dead they smoked
and talked of the night ahead

the thousandth corpse burst apart
and its fermented guts ruined the only
clothes of two of the men
around them the others stood
frozen and helpless
in the face of this tragedy

c.

it was the time of the living dead
who for reasons ill-understood
congregated in the disused stations
and bus depots of the remaining cities
perhaps they had always been there
with their blank unseeing stares
they were impossible to move along
and none of them would explain their presence
if moved they returned to the spot
they had been moved from

frantic security officials reasoning
that these intractable individuals
were waiting for a train or bus home
managed to drum up some transport
but the living dead were unwilling
to board the wrong bus it seemed
to those delegated to deal with them
that they were waiting for normal
services to resume unwilling to learn
that many of their houses birthplaces
and beloved family members were vaporised
or underneath several meters of seawater

in the end they were left by themselves
in their hundreds sleeping on the seats
which had been designed in the early eighties
to discourage sleeping and similar
disreputable non-consumer activities
whenever it was possible to divert food
they were fed until the lack of sanitation
slaughtered the majority of them during the third
inexplicably hot summer

d.

By the time that it was thought
to requisition horses
to facilitate communication
between the major centres remaining
most of them had been eaten
rumours came of a surviving herd
somewhere in Yorkshire so
a small party of officers
set out to investigate
third day out
their jeep was stolen as
they stopped to ask directions
along with all their food and
most of their weapons
but they pressed on
they were hungry footsore
and circling Hull
or whatever was there now
when the great blizzard hit them
eight of them were lost in the

four meter drifts and the other's lost
toes, fingers and a nose as their
feet and hands blackened

when the survivors began to lose their teeth
they would have turned back but they did not
know which way to turn
the wind had become such that the snow
would not lie but blew like grit
pitting numb flesh through their rags
even if there had been something to see
they were all half blind in the storm
but suddenly up upon a ridge
right in front of them surrounded
by a golden glow which
must have been the sun seeping through
the clouds weakly like turmeric
spreading in the yogurt of a thick curry
for so their thoughts were running
in silhouette stood a proud horse
mane and tail streaming like silk
in the gale they stopped still
catching that beast was absolutely
out of the question

e.

gradually the battery-powered timepieces ran down
the clocks based on atomic decay were already forgotten
the sun came up climbed through the clouds and set again
no-one's wound watch agreed exactly punctuality became
approximate again people turned up on the right day
if they could decision-making slowed to the speed
of the seasons yet there was so much to be done

water had to be drawn from the well
after each rainfall the taster pig
was given a fresh bucket to drink
twice in the first five years
hog hair fell out and the taster lost weight
so the storage tank had to last for months
until the well had cleansed itself

unleavened bread was baked for yeast had become unstable
and at times rose up in the oven like detergent in water
bubbling explosively to collapse into char on the walls
but then sometimes it would rise the dough alright but
the taste was hard metallic like blood or magnesium
despite the efforts made to retain a pure strain
the yeast would not breed true in any home

because there could be no beer they
partied on marijuana and boiled water
stretching out the time during
a few hours for a wedding here a
death there a live birth occasionally
in between it killed pain eased the
hard slog and was grown out of old habit
in secret behind the church

NOW WHEN I WAS YOUR AGE

a.

We had silent machines to tell the time
some of them built to tick off
just to tick off each second's duration
every hour a bell was struck and
there were twenty-four hours in a day
time went on at work the hours were measured
as we stamped in and out
under lighting you cannot imagine
we did not see the seasons turning
and until I was twenty-one corn
came in flakes from a box

machines are things like the lorry
when it was still running and
you have seen clocks as we went through town
stopped though they were
cornflakes were made I think
like bread but much smaller
although my factory made lightbulbs
well it did not belong to me but I
why did I work there
well I got paid but no

not in corn I was paid cash in the hand
and then I'd stop off at the pub
for a quick one
no not a joint a pint
it had the same sort of effect
and they rang a bell for last orders too

b.

On a Friday we got done up to the nines
and went down the pub and maybe for a wee dance
later on it was grand then a few quid in
the fruit machine a few pints latest
sounds on the tape system eying the talent
and feeling on top of the world
the time passed too damn quick
before you knew it Monday was there again

no pints don't make the time pass
all by themselves it's like
you remember that bottle of wine we found
in the back of that old guy's cellar
remember whoever had been through before
had missed just the one in that dark corner
remember that red wine you pulled a face
at it but we shared it anyway well
beer was like wine it blurred the edges

and if you ask me why edges
had to be blurred in order to eye talent
I think it was because there was
all that choice and romance in the air
of those days while now in the hard grind

you know you marry when the bleeding starts
beget with child and depend on each other
for the work as much as the pleasures

but you want to know what a fruit machine was
it took your money but you might win money
maybe even more money than you put in
I suppose that does mean the money was worthless
we thought gambling like barter but riskier
no no pubs weren't dangerous nor machines
neither they were for pleasure so
why did I not like Mondays
it was the work I guess
lightbulb after lightbulb with never an idea
from one week's end to the other

c.

we rented a video machine and watched movies
late nights and at the weekends
horror was my favourite like Friday the 13th
parts one to five Halloween four or five of them too
all that stuff was quite fake rubber blood came
in bottles it wouldn't wack a good beheading

its hard to explain movies they were like
pictures photographs you've seen some of them
I don't know how they moved it was not magic
but machinery the actors pretended
and the cameras rolled stopping when things
went wrong and doing them over it all sounds
quite senseless as I speak it all sounds so long ago

and now even those who can only write
must watch their words for fear that they offend
and oblige combat or banishment the video
makers would have been wandering this world in rags
come back Mad Max come back Howard the Duck
for the heroes have all been disembowelled for
failing to live up to their reputations to
the headman's satisfaction and the crazy
novelist up in the cave eating little
watching the shadows play above her head
she can go to hell while we get on with it
out in the real world of dirt and corn
no-one here even knows I can spell my name

d.

I had never drawn blood
in anger nor in friendship when
the doctor raised a sample from
my elbow with a needle I passed
cold flat out how about that
and now look here at my scars

So I learned of violence the hard way
in fear during the time when
only those afraid to die lived
when many believed that they were already dead
and in truth many were
I watched my lover bruise and fall apart
like an old banana
fought off those who wished to replace him
with the hammer in our cellar

until he died and I wondered
how had I lived so long

But you cannot beat yourself to death
so I came up into the light
walked north and here I am
later you were born
during the first winter
I killed a man who would
eat you and we lived from his flesh
though I bore him no grudge
no one knows of it

e.

No-one stood guard in the night
we locked the doors and went to bed
secure in our insurance that
someone would pay for whatever went wrong
now here we are a mother
a child and a gun

but the night is short when you talk
and you have the heart of a lion
I cannot see you in those days
I cannot see you in a bedroom
with pandas on the wallpaper
I cannot see you at your lessons
in a classroom of silence
for here you are sleeping the
night watch away with me
your golden penumbra of hair
against the dawn my warrior
my child of the future

will you watch for me
on a hilltop some night
will you dream of me when I am dust
and speak of me when you have
shut the door on the past
finally or at least
croon the tunes I have sung to you

COPING WITH STRESS - A SEMINAR

a.

the saxophone man is coming to town
blowing his breathy tunes of the old days
valves controlled with knicker-elastic
until he can get to a soldering-iron
pockets full of wooden reeds shaved
by a sharp knife and wound with cotton
when he gets to the square he lets
the horn slip back on its strap and
to the strummed strings of a small guitar
sings of the news from outside from
over the hills from the South
from Africa itself so he tells us all

when he first came by small children
ran in tears at the man with
the screaming snake reflecting fire
hanging from his mouth
but they are over that now
and they follow him to town
clapping along to the tunes

which he blows so well
they have never heard anything like it

there is one old chap in the village
who swears that he used to play the horn
himself until he lost a hand along with his wife
and wandered away up here now
he wields a scythe with one-armed grace
cutting silage for Mr. Smith who
himself patrols the perimeter with a shotgun
the saxophone man remembers them all
and especially the widow
- what a silly word in this time
but her husband died Afterwards -
who he sleeps with here

she tells him the news
six infants lost this winter
and old Mrs McTavish of bronchitis
whose toothless widower
will later slip your man
two coils of copper wire to sound
a lament over her wooden cross
for the occasion beneath the stars
of a late frost he blows
an old tune that maybe
no-one else alive knows
'The Stopper' by Sonny Rollins
Mr McTavish listens impassively
"she would have liked that she would"
he says "always was partial
to that country and western

what was it called again"
"Nevada Sundown" says the
saxophone man and shivering in his best shirt
heads back to the widow's arms

b.

by the beating of a hammer
a hammer on the metal girder
beating ringing from the square
so the township is assembled
so that they can see the trial
they are trying some strange man
whom was found in Jimmy's field
busy eating Jim's potatoes
Jim is angry Jim wants death Jim
would have done him in himself
if an he had caught the bastard
the starving stranger will say nothing
nothing gained the verdict's certain

his head comes off clean and
the spigot of blood is licked eagerly
by dogs it is said that
in some parts he would have been eaten

here with heavy intonation
holding up the Highway Code
revised published 1987 by HMSO
the headman hammers the head
hammers the head hard onto a pole
a pole which beside Jim's field
by the field will call the crows

away from crops and to the skull
the townsfolk dance the townsfolk chant
kids strip the clothes and
the body goes down the shithole
someone blags his nuts for charms

c.

the weather woman says
i need a lot of money now fast
and you will get a big crop
coming in damn soon
fuck the clouds that you see
and look to those in your heart

the weather woman thumbs
certified plastic script and
hollers her god-found song
man she ripped me off cos
the rains come and do
my barley low so
here i stole her song

the weather woman sings
fly high cloud
fly on high
fly high cloud
fly on by

oh i seen you were a bird
oh i laid you out the seed
oh i know you were the sun's
breath
fly on high

fly high cloud
fly on high
fly high cloud
bye bye bye

the weather woman sweats
like cheese in her horse skin skirt
she don't know i stole her song
as she can't read nor write
just as well for she got
the power to rip my
learned guts apart
still gives me the bad eye
as she splits

d.

this kid yells
right as it pops
before even it
gets the slap
she's pretty
straight but
for that yell
she's pretty

first proper kid
that's dropped all year
we'll make her baby name
Prima till we find
how she turns out
let her be primo
let her be whole
let her be of us

after that first yell
she stays quiet
for the whole five days
that she survives
so that name won't be
given around here
again for a while

e.

this is the first blood tale
the first blood words of Kevin
J. Mitchell
this is how it was

when they came they came
a horde of them came
over the hill the hill there
yelling aloud yelling their death songs
man they had guns they had
a rocket launcher when the
first cottage burst in flame
many brave men shit their pants
but I threw my spear hard
it sank hard into the leg
of the savage with the rocket
he screamed like a rabbit
as he screamed I charged and
split his head
the shitpants followed me they
followed me and the rats fled
back over the hill the hill
there where they came from

later we burned their lairs
stole nine horses

that is how it was
every word I speak is truth
on my Mother's blood.

LEADERSHIP POTENTIAL

a.

so many words have been written and spoken
that the different clans
no longer share their meaning
on a midsummer salvage trip
to the old flooded city
they meet in suspicion
but sit weapons laid aside
and speak in mime and sign

holding up a book

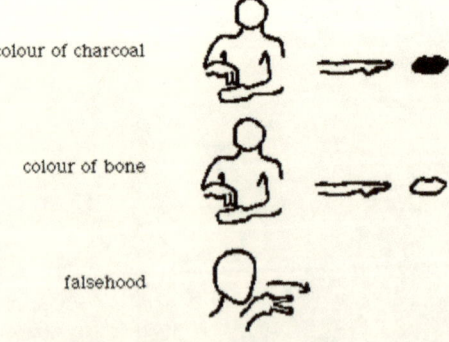

b.

such things cannot be trusted
or traded they have no need
for each other yet are
these civil words wasted?

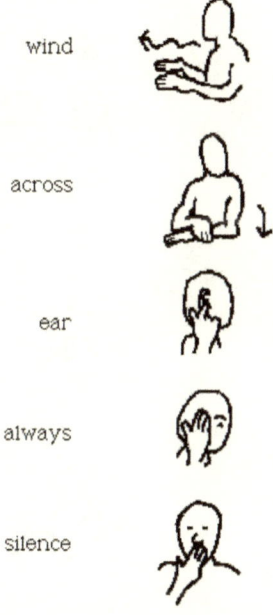

wind

across

ear

always

silence

c.

with nothing left to be said
they would leave
but an old man
tongue fallen still
in the land of dreams
has his turn

RICHARD HAMMERSLEY: BORDERS POETRY

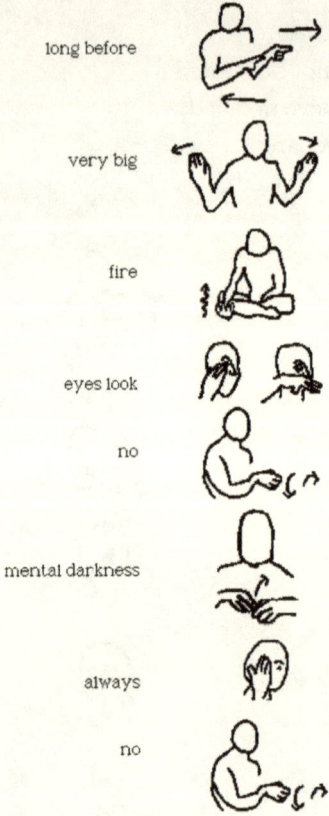

long before

very big

fire

eyes look

no

mental darkness

always

no

d.

too young to remember
they see in each other
identical needs and wants
without further discussion
some gather wild barley
others share jerky

good

work

together

speak

exchange

spirit

e.

and what of the future
well who can say for certain
   but

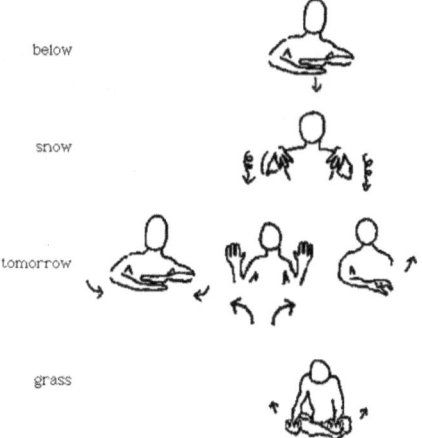

below

snow

tomorrow

grass

RICHARD HAMMERSLEY: BORDERS POETRY

TO RECAP

the little random creatures

found a hole with a light in it, and saying
Whose?
    set a trap
with a bowcord for a noose.
A giant of light, something alive, dazzled the path
on its slow way up, blinding
the little random creatures
o something alive was dying in the bowcord and it said
    Allow me to choke to death
    And you'll have night forever
and they let the sun go

                              Fox narrative.

NOTES

A work of this length may benefit from some hints concerning its construction. It is "about" both the threat of global catastrophe and the nature of the imagination. Ambiguities resound throughout it. The appeal of a great disaster seems to me to have been under-appreciated. For, disasters upend the material world and make our hidden values real. Ach, the material world, we cannot bear it and we cannot survive without it. That is the nature of this poem.

To maintain the fluidity and freshness of speech this work is written in idealised British speech patterns, without consideration for conventional rules of syntax or rhythm. Since William Carlos Williams, poetry which has used speech-based feet has often been confused with free verse or accused of being prose chopped up at random. The poem does not dance to a rock-steady count but it still has rhythm. The speech patterns move from oral narrative to bureaucratic pronouncement and back again to oral narrative. This movement extrapolates a tendency which already exists to render current affairs as myths for popular consumption. In the end those myths will be all that exist.

In the writing of this work I sense the poetic influences of Bertold Brecht, William Carlos Williams & Jerome Rothenberg, but not, I admit, much influence from modern British writing. Perhaps it is appropriate that a poem about the end of the United Kingdom as we know it should be written outside the mainstream of British poetry. That mainstream seems to me to be academic - drawing upon a university-taught body of English literature - and metaphorical - writing about things which stand for other things, rather than about the things themselves. In contrast, this writing tries to be populist - drawing upon contemporary culture - and exemplarily - writing about things by describing examples of those things. By this approach I have hoped to avoid cleverness and obscurity and provide a poetry which is accessible and relevant without a literary education. But all things will pass...

Glasgow 1986 (amended 1991)

PREVIOUS PUBLICATION

Unlock the hidden powers of your mind, part e., Sufficient emergency security measures, part a. and Leadership potential, parts a. & d.; Samzstat 1(1), 1986.

Now when I was your age; The West Coast Magazine 1(1) 1988.

I had a nightmare and there is a lot of living in fear; in a booklet accompanying the Mayfest New Poets reading at the Third Eye Centre, Glasgow, 1986.

Acknowledgments

The Kafka quote on page 3 is from At Night translated by Tarina & James Stern; from The Complete Stories edited by N.N. Glatzer, Schocken Books, New York, 1983.

The sign language in "Leadership potential" is adapted from Indian Sign Language by Robert Hofsinde, Morrow, New York, 1956.

the little random creatures is Armand Schwerner's working of a Fox narrative - after William Jones; from Shaking the Pumpkin, edited by Jerome Rothenberg, Doubleday, New York, 1972.

ABOUT THE AUTHOR

Richard Hammersley is a health psychologist who had a long university career and still practices from his family home in the Scottish Borders. He also spends time in the East Riding of Yorkshire. He is very happily married and has four amazing daughters.

He started writing poetry aged 13, inspired partly by Bob Dylan and partly because he thought writing a poem for English homework at school was easier than writing a whole story. Whilst studying for his PhD in Cambridge he was a member of the Cambridge Poetry Society, Secretary of the Cambridge Poetry Festival, made concrete and sound poetry, published his first small lobby press book, co-edited 'Perfect Bound' and took poetry so seriously that if he hadn't got his first academic job, at University of California San Diego where he attended poetry seminars and sessions at the Center for Music Experiment, then he was considering becoming a poet, whatever that would have meant at the time; probably a more pedestrian day job than being a psychologist and university teacher. He has published and performed in various places over the years, occasionally even getting paid, and he has never stopped writing.

www.ingramcontent.com/pod-product-compliance
Lightning Source LLC
LaVergne TN
LVHW041248080426
835510LV00009B/643